BEING YOUR CAT

BEING YOUR CAT

What's really going on in your feline's mind

Celia Haddon
Dr Daniel Mills FRCVS

First published in Great Britain in 2023 by Cassell, an imprint of
Octopus Publishing Group Ltd
Carmelite House, 50 Victoria Embankment,
London EC4Y 0DZ
www.octopusbooks.co.uk

An Hachette UK Company
www.hachette.co.uk

Distributed in the US by Hachette Book Group
1290 Avenue of the Americas, 4th and 5th Floors,
New York, NY 10104

Distributed in Canada by Canadian Manda Group
664 Annette St., Toronto, Ontario, Canada M6S 2C8

ISBN 978 1 78840 405 1

A CIP catalogue record for this book is available from the British Library.

Printed and bound in UK

1 3 5 7 9 10 8 6 4 2

Typeset in 12/19pt Sabon LT Pro by Jouve (UK), Milton Keynes

Publisher: Trevor Davies
Senior Managing Editor: Sybella Stephens
Copy Editor: Robert Anderson
Proofreader: Caroline Taggart
Assistant Production Manager: Emily Noto

This FSC® label means that materials used for
the product have been responsibly sourced.

Dedicated to my amazingly tolerant wife Connie, and all the cats she has introduced me to over the years. I've learned so much from all of you.

—Daniel Mills

CONTENTS

Introduction: What is it like to be your cat?   1

1   What it is like being in your feline body   13
2   How your ancestors became pets   31
3   What it is like being a kitten   49
4   What you see and hear as a cat   67
5   What you smell, taste and touch as a cat   85
6   How you talk as a cat – with sound,
    body language and touch   103
7   How as a cat you talk with scent – your
    secret language   119
8   What it is like to feel feline emotions   135
9   What it is like to think as a cat   153
10 What it is like being a rescue cat   171
11 What it is like being a pet   187
12 What you as a cat want – choice
    and control   205

Appendix 1: Useful organizations, websites and
    other resources   211
Appendix 2: The mysteries of cat behaviour   213
Endnotes   221
Index   239
Acknowledgements   247
Picture credits   248

INTRODUCTION: WHAT IS IT LIKE TO BE YOUR CAT?

What is it like to see the world through your cat's eyes, hear the world through feline ears, smell the world through your cat's nose, taste food the way it tastes to your cat, and feel the world through your cat's whiskers?

It's a very different world from the human world.

Different types of animal, different species, live in different worlds. Indeed, each species has its own senses and biases in its brain, and experiences the world according to what is important for its survival. No creature can experience all reality. The brain leaves out what is not necessary for the lifestyle of each animal, either blanking it out completely, or blurring it, as it were, into the background. The brain also groups other things together according to what is important to it: for example, all those things that are to be avoided. But what makes up that category varies from one species to another. We all live in our own realities, allowing us to focus on what matters and discarding the rest. This applies as much to humans as it does to cats.

To understand your cat, therefore, you need to know the basis of the world that it lives in, because a cat's world is so different from your world. And for that you need a guidebook – this book – to get a better understanding of the feline world.

Humans live in a world with a concave blue sky, the sight of hills in the distance miles away in the landscape, and the faint smell of the roses in the garden; younger individuals with good hearing may just be able to detect the cry of a bat on a summer evening. The landscape that the cat sees and the soundscape that the cat hears are very different. The human smellscape and the feline smellscape are (as one might say) worlds apart. Many of the odours in the world do not register strongly in the human brain at all – the smell of a mouse dropping left 12 hours ago, for example, or the odour of next door's dog lifting its leg on the front doorstep, or the curious plastic smell given off by an electric plug heating up. These scents belong to the world of the cat, where they are very significant. Conversely, the cat world has no bright blue sky or accurate distant landscapes. These are blurred out.

YOUR CAT'S UMWELT

There's a word for these different realities – *umwelt*. Translated literally from the German this means 'environment'. But ethologists – those who study the natural behaviour of animals – use it to describe the world as it is experienced by a particular living organism: the self-world of an animal. The writer who first used the word in this particular sense was Professor Jakob Johann von Uexküll (1864–1944), a Baltic German aristocrat whose family lost their fortune in the 1917 Russian Revolution. To support himself he became an academic biologist. His theory of umwelt can be summed up this way: 'All animals, from the simplest to the most complex, are fitted into their unique worlds with equal completeness.'[1]

The example he gave was the world of the tick. Ticks are tiny eight-legged creatures, related to spiders, that attach themselves to animals to suck their blood. They look like a small round bag with legs and a beak at the front. Hikers with bare legs may find a tick on their leg, and if they are unwise enough to squash it, the tick will not only empty out the bag of blood all over their fingers but leave behind its mouthparts, which can carry the nasty bacterium that causes Lyme disease.

So what is the world, the umwelt, of this tick?

Von Uexküll described the simple life cycle of the tick. A female tick climbs upwards to the tip of a twig or a blade of grass. She climbs upwards, not downwards, towards the light, light that she senses through her skin. Then, if she detects the odour of a warm-blooded animal – the smell of butyric acid which exudes from the skin glands of all mammals – she hurls herself towards it. If she lands on the prey, she knows she is in the right place because the animal is warm. If she misses the animal and lands on the cold ground, she has to start to climb again. Once on the animal, she wriggles through the fur till she finds a hairless bit of skin, then sticks her mouth through the skin to suck the warm blood. Full of blood, she falls to the ground, lays her eggs and dies. As von Uexküll pointed out: 'Experiments . . .have proved that the tick lacks all sense of taste. Once the membrane is perforated, she will drink any fluid of the right temperature.'[2]

The world of a tick, her umwelt, is therefore a simple but effective one. To survive, a tick does not need to see well, feel much or smell much – just the things that help her survive. The smell of a rose or wet grass is not part of her world. There is no bright blue canopy of the sky for the tick. She has no sense of taste because she doesn't need one. The noise of the passing animal on to which she will drop is silent for her because she has no hearing. In her world, there are only a few things that she perceives or needs to perceive – the light towards which she climbs on the blade of grass, the odour of the passing animal, the tactile sensation as she lands on then burrows through the hair of a furry animal, and the warmth of the blood which is her meal. Only these stimuli have what Jakob von Uexküll described as 'a special biological meaning' for her. He added: 'The whole rich world around the tick shrinks and changes into a scanty framework . . .her umwelt. But the very poverty of this world guarantees the unfailing certainty of her actions . . .'[3]

Cats are not ticks, although ticks sometimes fall on them! There is more, much more, in their world, but it is a different world from that of a human.

WALKING IN YOUR CAT'S PAWS

Can we really put ourselves into our cat's world? Walk through the house in their paws? See with their eyes? Hear with those feline ears?

Philosophers and biologists have debated whether we can ever get into the mind of another person, let alone a cat. Do we even know what our human partner or our child is thinking? Of course, we can ask them and, if they answer truthfully, we can get some idea. But maybe even then what they tell us and how they describe their thoughts and feelings will only convey to us what we personally are able to imagine – not the full reality of their inner world as they experience it, but only our version of it.

We can never feel the exact feelings or think the exact thoughts of another human being any more than we can completely feel their bodily feelings of pain if they fall over on a concrete pavement. We can imagine what those feelings and thoughts might be like, and then with empathy feel what we would feel if we were in their place. Even so, this will never be exactly what another human experiences. We can imagine the pain of that fall on concrete, but only as we would feel it, not as they feel it. Other minds are never wholly open to us.

So how on earth can we know what it is like to be one of our cats? Is it even possible?

The American philosopher Thomas Nagel (1937–) wrote a famous essay, 'What is it like to be a bat?', in which he grappled with the difficulty of what it is like to try to be in another being's mind, in particular in an animal's mind:

> Conscious experience . . .occurs at many levels of animal life, though we cannot be sure of its presence in the simpler organisms, and it is very difficult to say in general what provides evidence of it . . .The fact that an organism has conscious experience at all means, basically, that there is something it is like to be that organism.[4]

He chose to write about bats because they are warm-blooded animals like ourselves but the way they 'see' their world through echolocation (a bit like radar) and the life they lead are so very different from humans. As he declared, 'Bat sonar, though clearly a form of perception, is not similar in its operation to any sense that we possess and there is no reason to suppose that it is subjectively like anything we can experience . . .'⁵ He concluded that we cannot even imagine what it would be like to have bat sonar. And even if we could imagine ourselves flying around in the dark catching insects with the help of high-frequency sound signals or hanging upside down to sleep, it would only tell us what it would be like for a human to do that; this is what some blind individuals have learned when they use echoes to help them navigate environments. However, using their experience as an equivalent to that of a bat is still anthropomorphic – that is, attributing human experience to a non-human animal. The world of the bat remains essentially closed to us, Nagel declared, no matter how well we research its life. Indeed, he claimed that science itself cannot help us with some parts of reality such as the inner experience of a bat.

So where does this leave you if you want to understand fully the life of your cat?

Should you just learn the biological and behavioural facts and leave it at that? Is anything other than hard facts – the results of scientific endeavour – dangerously anthropomorphic? Should we cat lovers give up trying to imagine what it is like to be a cat? Most scientists studying animal behaviour are, rightly, wedded to the idea that the simplest explanation for any animal behaviour should usually be chosen over a more complex one. This is known as Morgan's Canon, after the psychologist Conwy Lloyd Morgan (1852–1936). It says: 'In no case is an animal activity to be interpreted as the outcome of the exercise of a higher psychical faculty, if it can be fairly interpreted as the outcome of the exercise of one which stands lower in the psychological scale.'⁶

But, of course, as Thomas Nagel pointed out, this is just a rule of thumb, because the complete experience of the inner life of an animal remains hidden from us anyway, hidden even from the most dedicated researcher. Some scientists, anxious to stick to what can be observed and proved, have gone even further. They have claimed that, while they see and measure animal and human behaviour, what is going on inside the animal is just impossible to know. It is either not worth knowing or simply is not there. The great American behaviourist B F Skinner (1904–90) studied how animals learned behaviour, working in his laboratory mostly with rats and pigeons, rather than cats. He could measure what they did but he could not, and did not try to, see or measure how they felt while they were doing it. He would train a rat to press a lever, for instance, and reward it for doing so with some food. The rat quickly learned that the consequence of pressing the lever resulted in the reward, and therefore repeated its behaviour. Skinner is one of the fathers of learning theory, and his findings have influenced all animal trainers who train with rewards, even if they do not know the theory behind their skill in training.

What might have been going on inside the brain of one of Skinner's rats? Did the rat feel pleasurable desire in the anticipation of getting the food? Was that pleasurable desire in its brain the reason why it pressed the lever? Did it feel frustration if the reward was not forthcoming, which in turn motivated it to try harder? Such questions were not for B F Skinner. He declared: 'The "emotions" are excellent examples of the fictional causes to which we commonly attribute behaviour.'[7] Just because he could strip something down to simple visible behaviour associations in the lab did not mean it was a simple process in the rat's brain. Though Skinner might be horrified by the very idea, these brain processes include consciousness – that is, how the world is experienced.

DO ANIMALS HAVE AN INNER LIFE?

The view that animals may not have inner lives has a long history. It goes back to the 17th century when some philosophers and scientists believed that animals were merely like machines as they had no souls. An extreme version of this standpoint was taken by the French rationalist and priest Nicolas Malebranche (1638–1715), who wrote:

> In dogs, cats, and other animals, there is neither intelligence nor a spiritual soul in the usual sense. They eat without pleasure; they cry without pain; they believe without knowing it; they desire nothing; they know nothing; and if they act in what seems to be an intelligent and purposive manner, it is only because God has made them fit to survive and has constructed their bodies in such a way that they can organically avoid – without knowing that they do so – everything that might destroy them and that they seem to fear.[8]

Nowadays there are very few biologists who would go so far as Malebranche or even agree with Skinner. Neuroscience has changed everything. We can now look at the workings inside the brain and see emotional networks in action. In July 2012 a group of cognitive neuroscientists declared: 'The weight of evidence indicates that humans are not unique in possessing the neurological substrates that generate consciousness. Non-human animals, including all mammals and birds, and many other creatures, including octopuses, also possess these neurological substrates.'[9] This declaration says that animals have some kind of consciousness, and it would be harder today to find a biologist who claims that our cats have no inner lives, that they are simply furry automata.

Even so, we must accept that we cannot ever fully put ourselves into our cats' experience of life. If so, is there any point in at least trying to imagine what it is like to be a cat? Does it matter if we are being anthropomorphic in doing this?

Concern for animal welfare is why we should do it. Fellow feeling, a form of anthropomorphism, promotes animal welfare. It helps us better care for animals. If we believe animals are just machines without feelings, we will feel free to cause them pain. If we believe they, like us, can suffer pain and have rich emotional lives, we will treat them better. If we can imaginatively put ourselves into the world of a cat, using the information that science has given us, we can appreciate how things that might be irrelevant or harmless to us might have real meaning to them and so better understand how we can give our cats a better life. Sadly, a lot of suffering occurs when people do not make the additional step of trying to put themselves in the experiential world of another, but merely ask how they would feel (as a human) in that situation.

Honest empathy motivates kindness. A study of psychology students showed that when they read a text in which dogs were described in anthropomorphic language, they were more ready to help dogs than when they had read a text describing dogs in non-anthropomorphic language.[10] Strange? Not really. Most of us pet owners talk to our cats and dogs as if they were human listeners and feel they are part of the family. These anthropomorphic feelings are at least part of the reason why most of us would be horrified if our loved pet animal were served up as Sunday dinner.

We humans have many characteristics in common with cats and other mammals. We have the same warm-blooded body with similar organs. We have brains that follow a similar broad structure, even if some parts are relatively bigger in one species than the other. Even though we do not know for sure, most neuroscientists also think that our cats, like other mammals, have the capacity to feel emotions that in some ways, at least, are similar to human emotions.

Anthropomorphism, of course, can go too far – when we think other animals have the same priorities and desires for luxuries that we might have. Think of people who you sometimes see in a town street pushing their dog in a pram as if it were a human baby (not because it has mobility problems). That dog would probably much prefer to be down at pavement level, using its nose to scent out urine marks from other dogs and cocking its leg to add its mark to those on the lamp post. Or take a look at cats dressed up as human characters on the internet. Most do not look happy. A more subtle form of anthropomorphic failure is to feed cats from bowls lined up close to each other. This looks cute to us humans, who sit down to have a meal together as a social event, but it is often stressful for the cats. We humans will eat and drink in a line at a bar and enjoy the sociability that goes with this. Cats are generally not sociable in their eating habits. They usually prefer to eat alone. Almost certainly, at least some of the cats in the line will be anxious at having to eat so close to another cat.

These are the mistakes of anthropomorphism arising from our love and emotional engagement with cats. They often occur out of good intention but also out of ignorance. Knowledge helps us avoid these mistakes. Using science to test ideas and try to understand the world from that animal's perspective and the environment it has adapted to live in is an example of what is known as *critical anthropomorphism* and is an important skill for researchers and owners alike.

We can use our imagination to light up knowledge and create the empathy that motivates us to do the best we can for our animals.

For example, all of us know that domestic cats are much smaller than human beings. That is obvious even to the human who dislikes felines. Yet how many of us have thought through the implication of being a small animal? What does being small mean in a world inhabited by much larger animals, some of them hostile to cats? How does a cat feel when a gigantically heavy human it them and hugs it tight against their giant chest? If we use our imagination, we should be able to see that for many cats this could be a frightening, rather than a pleasant, experience. That may encourage us to express our affection in a more acceptable form, if we really care about cats.

If we fuse imagination with knowledge, using the available science and an honest approach to empathy to understand them, we will get a much better understanding of the feline umwelt. However, we must be humble and admit that we will still make some mistakes. Nonetheless, this all helps us to practise a more thoughtful and kindlier care for our cats.

Put yourself in the place of your cat and enter its umwelt – its secret world.

1

WHAT IT IS LIKE BEING
IN YOUR FELINE BODY

When you first inhabit your feline body, you notice a strange sensation. You can feel fur under your chin and cheek, and all over your body. If you are curled up and resting, your face will be positioned on your tail, which is also furry. Your tail is curved round over your back legs, forming a cosy cushion for your head. This is the first experience of your new feline body – covered with fur and with an entirely new appendage, the tail.

Then you stretch. Humans who do yoga or Pilates stretch this way deliberately. But you just do it automatically. Your back rides high up, and your four legs stiffen. Four of them. Then you lean forwards to stretch the back legs. The stretch flows through you in a delicious way, without you having to think about what you are doing or what you need to do next. Your whole body has a kind of effortless grace. You realize you have no hands. Just legs. This is the second experience of your new feline body.

ON FOUR LEGS

Four legs make a huge difference. The template for a mammal, whether a human or a cat, is more or less the same body framework, with an approximately similar skeleton, but in each species the design is modified to fit what the individual species needs in its environment. As the famous naturalist Charles Darwin (1809–92) wrote: 'What can be more curious than that the hand of a man, formed for grasping, that of a mole for digging, the leg of a horse, the paddle of the porpoise and the wing of the bat, should all be constructed on the same pattern.'[1] This similar pattern, modified to each species, applies to both the human and the cat.

BONES IN THE FELINE BODY

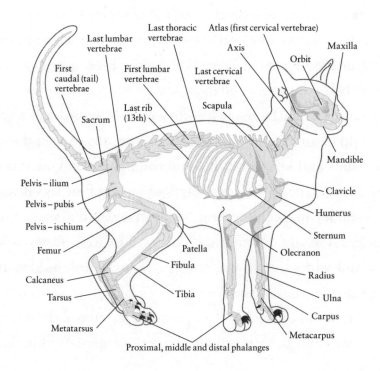

Last thoracic vertebrae · Atlas (first cervical vertebrae)
Last lumbar vertebrae · Axis · Maxilla
First caudal (tail) vertebrae · First lumbar vertebrae · Last cervical vertebrae · Orbit
Sacrum · Last rib (13th) · Scapula · Mandible
Pelvis – ilium · Clavicle
Pelvis – pubis · Humerus
Pelvis – ischium · Sternum
Femur · Patella · Olecranon
Calcaneus · Fibula · Radius
Tarsus · Tibia · Ulna
Metatarsus · Carpus
Metacarpus
Proximal, middle and distal phalanges

If you are a cat, this framework is mainly horizontal rather than vertical. This horizontal skeletal pattern, common to many animals, changes everything. Your spine, which in humans is swivelled back vertically, with the body weight supported entirely on the two legs, is now carried horizontally like a bridge by your four legs. Your arms are now your front legs, and your back legs are much shorter than the long human legs. Unlike the hoofed animals, your five digits (in humans, the fingers) are still separate, although the dew claw of the front paw is very small. You only have four toes on the back legs because the fifth toe is so vestigial that it has no claw and is usually invisible.

Your body weight is borne by the four toes of the four feet. Other animals may have more stamina in their forelimbs, but your forelimbs are designed for bursts of speed and quick acceleration. Your paws, with their specialized retractable claws, are mobile enough to grasp prey, to swat opponents, to climb trees and to act as a comb in grooming.[2]

Your body is steadier and more stable than a human body. A cat never has to balance on one leg, for example. In order to imagine the world of an animal with four legs, humans can get down on their hands and knees. But it is not the same as having four legs for walking. One of the advantages of having four legs is that, if you lose a leg in a car accident, you can learn to manage fine on three legs. Cats do not need crutches or false legs. Tanny, a feisty black-and-white kitten, was found in a farmyard, hidden away, waiting to die from a smashed front leg. The finder took her to the local vet. Within hours of the operation to remove the damaged leg, she was able to totter round the vet's surgery. Within days of being fostered by her new owner, Celia, she could jump and play like any normal kitten. After a few weeks with her new owners, they photographed her high up in a tree. She had climbed up easily on her three remaining legs, another advantage of having four legs to begin with.

CAT AGILITY

So, as a cat you will run faster, accelerate more quickly, jump higher, turn and twist more easily, and balance better, because of your four legs and flexible spine. You can jump very high from a standing start. You can leap high into the air to clear the top of long grass and complete an airborne front-foot pounce to pin down your prey. You can walk, trot or canter and also slowly crawl in a crouching posture low to the ground. These abilities are necessary for a hunter stalking its prey or slipping away from a predator in the undergrowth. The slow crouching retreat of a cat is sometimes nicknamed 'moon walking'. What you lose with the lowered body position is the ability to trot steadily for very long distances, like dogs or wolves that need to track and chase down their prey, often for a long time.[3] Your feline stealthy stalk takes extra energy because your legs cannot be efficiently swung like a pendulum.

The major disadvantage of four legs is that you do not have the front legs free to use as hands. True, you can pounce on prey, using the front paws to pin down a mouse. You can swipe with a single paw, leaving all the other three legs on the ground. You can poke with a front paw. You can, if you have an owner who teaches tricks, sit back on your bottom and wave both front legs in a kind of high-five. You can even stand up on your two hindlegs to get a higher field of vision;

to look over high foliage, for instance. But you can only hold this position for a short relatively time.

Your human fingers are now the toes of your front paws. You walk on the four toes of each foot, instead of both toes and heels being flat on the ground like a human. The human stance is plantigrade; yours is digitigrade – that is, you are standing on your digits, your toes. If a cat starts walking in a flat-footed way on the centre or back of their paws, not on the toes, it is often a sign of diabetic neuropathy or a ruptured tendon.

Above your feline toes in the front leg are the metacarpal bones which stretch upwards from the paw pads. In humans, these bones are flat in the palm of the hand. The central pad of your paw is known as the metacarpal pad. Your feline wrist joint comes next and is relatively higher up towards the trunk of the body than in a human and marked by the carpal, or stopper, pad – so called because it can help you suddenly stop or reduce sliding when going down a slope. Your elbow is where the front leg appears to join the body. In your back legs, the ankle is where the leg hinges backwards and the knee is level with where the back leg joins the body. Forelegs and hindlegs have a different structure and a different function. About 60 per cent of your weight, according to one estimate, is carried by your front legs, while your back legs, which are longer, propel your body forwards, upwards and over objects.[4]

Walking on tiptoes has advantages. Your paw pads are made up of elastic and collagen fibres with fatty tissue acting as a kind of shock-absorbing cushion when you jump down from a height. These hairless cushioned pads, with hair and glands in between them, also help to keep your tiptoe walk silent, which is particularly useful for stalking prey. You walk lightly over the world – far more silently than humans can – partly because of this tiptoe anatomy and partly because you are so much lighter.

Like other, but not all, four-footed animals, your feline gait proceeds diagonally. In an ordinary walk, with most of your weight towards the front of your body, if the right front leg moves forward, the next leg to move is the left back leg. Each leg is placed on the ground at a regular but slightly different time in a so-called four-beat gait. Your hindfoot is placed almost on to the front paw print, and most of the time three legs are on the ground.[5] When you move fast, these diagonal leg movements are speeded up so that at moments only one or two legs may be on the ground or even all four legs momentarily in the air in a two-beat fast-gait canter or gallop. In a canter or a gallop, your hindlegs provide most of the force to speed forward in a leaping motion with the spine fully extended; then, with all four feet off the ground then compressed to bring your hindquarters under the body, your back legs touch the ground before pushing upwards again.

All this sounds complicated when it is written down, but will feel as natural to the feline you as walking or running on two legs feels to a human who has good balance. You do not have to look down to what your feet are doing as you move, for you have scanned the ground a little further forward than your front feet to see if there are obstacles. And, unlike humans, you can lower your body to stalk without having to crouch down and curve your spine.

Your feline paws are beautifully designed, too. The four digits of each fore and back paw are thicker than ordinary skin, as is the skin on human feet. But your pads are far more sensitive than the soles of human feet. One reason for this sensitivity is that the skin folds between your pads, where the hair grows, are dense with nerve endings called *touch domes*, specialized areas full of cells that detect the exact nature of the ground you are walking upon.

Cat toe pads are often affectionately nicknamed toe beans, because their cushioned surface is a little like a jellybean. Your feline fifth digit, the dew claw on the front paw, is higher up the front leg, like a kind of tiny thumb. It is not as useful as a human thumb – thus the joke that, if cats had thumbs, they would rule the world. Your dew claw does help, however, in climbing: it steadies the leg when it is in contact with the tree trunk. It can also help you hold down struggling rodents or flapping birds. In some dogs, the dew claw steadies the foot when cantering. The dew claw does not help a cantering cat, however. It is the carpal/stopper pad, higher up than the dew claw on the inside of your wrist, that can help you slow down when you have been moving at speed.

Usually, cats have five toes on each front foot and four toes on each back foot. Occasionally, cats are born with more than the usual 18 toes. If you have six toes on your front paws, they will make your front feet splay out when you walk. Some of the extra toes may be slimmer than a normal toe, and not all of them will have a claw in each toe, though they may still play havoc scratching the sofa. The record for toes on a single feline paw is nine, though some of these may be stumps without claws! Polydactyl cats – the word comes from the Greek for 'many' and 'finger' – were prized as ship's cats. They were thought to be better mousers and also more able to steady themselves on a rocking ship with their splayed-out paws. When Daniel was in veterinary practice in Plymouth, one of Britain's important port cities, he saw a lot of polydactyl cats, possibly the modern descendants of these long-ago ship's cats that were specially chosen by the Plymouth sailors for this useful trait.

YOUR CLAWS – PITONS AND WEAPONS

You have curved claws instead of flat nails. Human nails are static, cannot be moved and grow out of skin. Your claws grow out of the bone, which is why declawed cats lose the tip of their toes, not just the claw. You can protract your claws so that you can use them to hold on to surfaces, but at rest your claws are sheathed. They are retracted and sheathed, too, when you are walking or running (unlike a dog's), so they stay sharp, unlike the blunt, thicker canine claw. You cannot do as much with a paw as humans can with a hand, but you can do quite a lot. Paws with claws protracted can be used to pull items towards you and to scratch, in either defence or attack. Thanks to your curved claws, you can climb up a 90-degree-angle tree trunk by digging them into the bark. Only a completely smooth 90-degree angle would defeat you because of the lack of grip available. Some humans can climb trees using their hands and feet on the branches, but most find it difficult, if not impossible, to climb up a right-angle trunk without a branch to hold on to. Yet any healthy cat can shin up a tree in a trice. Humans use pitons (metal spikes driven into rock cracks by climbers): your claws are your pitons.

You can also weaponize your claws. Some cats pat their human's face affectionately, with sheathed claws, so that only the soft paw pad delicately touches the skin. But if they want a human or another cat to back off, they can do a swipe with the claws out. Those scratches are painful because the claws are so sharp. Human nails are inferior weapons for scratching because they are neither as sharp nor as strong as a feline claw. Human nails just grow continuously, and if by accident a human loses a nail, the exposed area underneath is painfully sensitive, until the new nail grows from the base. You have a new claw ready for action: when your old claw falls off, the new one is revealed underneath. This is one of several reasons why you scratch the furniture or a scratch post, to pull off the worn-out sheath of the claw to uncover the new one. Claw accidents can occur in cats, of course, when the toenails or dew claws are torn off prematurely. These are just as painful for cats as for humans, as there is a high nerve and blood supply to the base of the claw.

JUMPS AND WRIGGLES

Human legs are great for walking and running but not much use for jumping compared with your feline legs. The powerful muscles in your back legs mean that you can jump about six times or more your own height from a standing start. This feline take-off speed is impressive and explains how you are able to pounce up and over tall grass on to a small mouse hidden from sight. What are the mechanics of this high pounce? The jump starts with a deep crouch. Maybe you shift your weight a little from leg to leg. Then your forelegs move upwards, and your hindlegs explode into movement. At lift-off, the hip and knee are at a tight angle and to get the speed you need they extend and straighten. No human being could jump anything like six times his or her own height from a standing start.

You can also wriggle very low in a stalking posture, although it takes up quite a lot of energy. You can squeeze under the living-room furniture even when there is only a tiny a gap. A four-inch space is enough for the average-sized cat, and many cats can wiggle into a gap lower than this if they are motivated either by fear or by the hope of catching a mouse there. Your flexibility is amazing. The bones of your spine are only loosely connected with each other and are well cushioned, allowing them to bend freely, and you have more vertebrae than a human spine has. Most adult humans have only 24 flexing vertebrae because the bottom vertebrae have fused together. Your feline spine has 27 flexing vertebrae, and you have a varying number in your tail depending on its length. The extraordinary way in which you double up your body to groom between your thighs is just one example of your flexibility. Your feline spine is so flexible you can arch your back into a tight U shape. There is also another reason why you can squeeze your body into tight places. You do not have a fixed collarbone, as humans do. The human collarbone is attached to the shoulders on either side, bracing the arms into place either side of the chest. Your collarbone (or clavicle) is rudimentary, sometimes even absent, and is attached to the rest of the body by muscle, not ligament. This allows for a narrow chest and more flexibility. You can squeeze through narrow spaces in a way you could never do if a fixed collarbone was keeping your front shoulders apart.

TELLING TAILS

And, of course, if you are a cat, you have a tail. All we humans have is the invisible stump of a tail, three to five vertebrae fused together and folded inwards into the coccyx to help us sit. Feline tail length varies from no tail at all (and no tail vertebrae) in a Manx cat, through about seven vertebrae in a Manx stumpy with a short tail, to a normal cat's tail with 18–23 vertebrae depending on length. It may be a wonderful bushy tail with long wavy hair on it like a Maine Coon, or it may be a tail with short hair in a short-haired domestic moggy. As a cat, you can feel the world with your tail just as you can feel the world with the rest of your body. Moreover, your tail is very mobile.

The feline tail does not just hang limply. Special tendons and six pairs of muscles allow it to lift up, stiffen, move side to side, bend upwards and downwards, or draw down tight between the hindlegs. The tip of your tail can move in a different direction to the rest of it. Your expressive tail can quiver, flick, thrash widely side to side, stick up straight from its base, often with a little forward curve at the tip, or lift up and then curve down about a third of its length. It acts as a signal for communication and a counterweight for any sudden movement of the body, thereby helping you to balance. Before modern ethical standards were introduced, researchers studied cats and their tails, as the felines walked along a narrow beam that moved sideways.[6] Cats with their tails intact used the tail by moving it in the opposite direction to the beam, allowing their body to stay on the beam. The researchers then cut the nerves to the tail, so that the cat lost control of its movements and was more likely to fall off the beam completely.

Yes, your tail helps with balance, but it is not necessary for balance in all circumstances. In some animals, geckoes for example, the tail is essential for aerial righting, and the longer the gecko tail the better its balance. As a cat, you have the ability to right yourself when you are falling from a height. If it is just a short fall, however, there isn't time for you to twist your body into the right position. In a longer fall, if you are upside down, first you bend slightly in the middle of your body, tucking in the front legs and sticking out your back legs. This means that your head and then the front half of your body twist downwards while the back half is still pointing upwards. Then you straighten out your front legs ready for landing and tuck in your rear legs, so that the back half catches up and all four legs are pointing downwards. Manx cats without a tail or cats that have lost their tail in an accident do not have too much difficulty doing this manoeuvre. From birth, Manx cats have presumably learned by experience how to balance without a tail, developing better muscles for balance, or they may be anatomically slightly different with longer legs.[7]

Tails help, but the key to your feline excellent ability to balance is found in your inner ear and is called the *vestibular apparatus*. This is what allows you to walk along the top of a narrow fence or pick your way across a cluttered mantelpiece without disturbing any item (unless perhaps you choose to push over an ornament in order to get the attention of your human!). This apparatus includes three fluid-filled semi-circular canals lined with microscopic hairs, or cilia. Movements of the your feline head shift the fluid and the cilia, which in turn send signals to the brain and register the position of your head relative to gravity. Your outer ears, or pinnae, are superior to the usually immobile human ears. You can mobilize your ears, making them swivel up and down and backwards and forwards. Your ears also have a charming little folded area at the base, which is called a *Henry's pocket* or, in textbooks, the *cutaneous marginal pouch*. It is possible that this apparently ornamental pouch is useful for locating prey from the high-pitched ultrasounds they produce.

A HUNTER'S HEAD

Your feline skull, if you are an ordinarily shaped cat, not a flat-face Persian, has a longer muzzle than the human skull and eye sockets that are, relative to the skull size, far larger than human eye sockets. You do not have a forehead as a human does, because you do not have such a large brain. Humans have a large frontal cortex, used for complex thought, self-consciousness and language. Self-satisfied humans would argue that your smaller brain is inferior to theirs. It isn't. Your brain is excellently adapted to your lifestyle. You do your own thing perfectly well without the huge human forebrain and are free of the unnecessary worries it generates for humans. A cat that was busy with complex thought would not survive very well in its ecological niche. You as a cat need to act fast and think fast, especially to catch your prey – too much brain activity applied to making associations, while good for problem solving, would slow things down. After all, cats have spread all over the world, inhabiting areas where humans do not or cannot live, despite their big brain. Your feline brain is just different, and the design of your skull is adapted to it. For instance, your brain is far superior to a human brain in the part devoted to smell, the olfactory bulb.

Another design adaptation allows you to kill prey by a single bite rather than the repeated bites used, for instance, by wolves to bring down prey. Your jaw can open relatively wider than a human jaw, and your upper and lower jaw are joined by strong ligaments. Your jaws move up and down, but not sideways, so they are no good for chewing bones or grinding hard substances. Instead, the jaw and teeth are designed for slicing off lumps of flesh before swallowing these whole. Because you are a total carnivore, your teeth are adapted to eating the flesh of small animals' flesh, not plants – another reason why you do not need teeth that chew as human teeth do. Just like your teeth, your digestive tract is designed for eating meat, and so is a short one rather than the long one needed by animals that must digest fibrous cellulose because they feed on vegetation.

Your killing teeth are the long canines at the side of the jaw. These are the teeth that break the neck of a mouse with a lethal bite. Between these at the front are the small incisors (three either side, top and bottom). These smaller teeth are used for nibbling, grooming and shearing. Further back behind the canines are the premolar teeth with sharp edges to slice off flesh, and right at the back the molars. In all, there are 30 permanent teeth (12 incisors, 4 canines, 10 premolars with 6 on the top and 4 on the bottom, and 4 molars).

Like our human teeth, and unlike rodents' teeth, your teeth do not keep growing. You can, like humans, suffer from toothache and lose a tooth. In your case, this will occur when the surface or the root of your teeth become eroded. This is called *tooth resorption* and is very painful indeed. You will find it hurts to eat, and you may stop eating altogether until the tooth is extracted by a vet.

When you have lost a tooth, it is lost for ever, as there are no implants yet for cats. Tooth loss, if it affects the killer bite, is going to be serious for you if you are living in the wild and must catch rodents and other prey for a living. But do not fear. If you are a pet cat, you will manage well without teeth in old age. Humans are inclined to overfeed rather than underfeed their cats, so you will have plenty of easy meals. You will find you can manage to swallow your dry kibble whole. Wet food, so called because it has a higher moisture content and so comes in an envelope or a tin, can also be easily swallowed, by using your tongue to shovel it down your throat.

You can do this because the design of the feline tongue is extraordinary. It is covered in sharp spines called *papillae*, facing to the back of the throat.[8] These spines shovel food backwards so it can be swallowed. This design allows you to pull up water while lapping. The spines also act as a grooming tool. At the top of each papilla is a scoop shape with a hollow cavity which takes up saliva from the mouth and then releases it on to the hair. Of course, the ordinary surface of your feline tongue is wet with saliva, too, but it is the papillae that allow the saliva to penetrate deep into your fur to the skin underneath. This is easy for short-haired cats, but, if you are a long-haired cat, the papillae may not be able to reach the roots of your fur and you will be prone to matting. Why bother to groom like this? One reason is that the application of saliva allows you to thermoregulate, that is, to cool down in warm weather despite your furry coat. Spreading saliva on the fur lowers your temperature. A thermal camera has revealed that saliva deposited on cat fur could cool down the temperature by as much as 17 °C (63 °F).

FURRY FELINES

A fur coat, which some status-conscious humans yearn for, is yours for free. You have fur almost everywhere. Humans have hair on their heads and visible hair on their pits and pubes (armpits and pubic region), on their eyebrows and on their eyelids as eyelashes. They also spend time shaving off the stronger hair from embarrassing parts of their bodies! All the rest of the human body has hairs, too, except for the palms of the hands and the soles of the feet, but this hair is so wispy and short that it is often invisible. Humans are hairy but not furry. Now you have become a cat, you will never have to shave again, although your owner may need to brush you if you have long hair. There are a few exceptions to normal feline furriness. Humans have interfered with cat genetics and have bred 'hairless' breeds like the Sphynx. This breed has hair on its body, but the hair is short and downy like a peach.

Most cats have fur which covers the whole of their body, except for some areas like the nose and paw pads. You will usually have fur between your toes, unlike polar bears and rabbits which have hair all over their foot pads. Unlike horses which sweat through their hairy skin to cool down, as a cat you can largely sweat only through the skin of your hairless paw pads and nose area. When you sweat with anxiety at the vet's, you may therefore leave damp footprints on the examination table. The sweat glands on your body are mainly for protecting your coat but also convey chemical signals. Damp paw pads are a sign of heat or stress. These sweat areas do not have a lot of skin surface to help you cool down. So, as well as sweating, you cool yourself down by putting saliva on your fur when grooming, which is remarkably efficient. But if you are very hot or stressed, you may start to pant. Your body temperature is naturally higher than a human one at 38.3–39.2 °C (101–102.5 °F), which means you can tolerate heat a little better. When you start to pant from the heat, with short quick breaths and open mouth, it may be a sign that you are potentially dangerously overheating.

Apart from the lack of sweat glands in your furred skin, the fact that you are furry over most of your body gives you an advantage over humans. You do not need clothes, although some owners of hairless cats put jackets on them to keep them warm. Your hair regulates your temperature, standing out further in cold weather to prevent more heat escaping from your body. It also protects your skin from sunburn and skin cancer. Only white cats and cats with white facial areas where the skin is hairless, or cats with very thin hair, are normally at risk from these diseases. Conscientious owners should keep them out of the sun at midday and perhaps even put feline sunblock on them.

Your fur coat consists of several different kinds of hair. The whiskers, or vibrissae, on your muzzle and on the lower side of your legs are strong, long and very special (more on these later). Then you have guard hairs, which extend further out from an undercoat. These carry a lot of the colour cells and are thicker and stiffer than the softer, fluffier awn hairs in the undercoat beneath them. Finally, there are the vellus hairs that are found on the otherwise hairless Sphynx cats. Some areas of your body, like the belly and inside of the thighs, have thinner hair and in some feline breeds there are tufts of longer hair at the top of the outside ear, known to cat breeders as *lynx tipping*. The inside of your ears may also have noticeably longer hair in tufts which breeders call *ear furnishings*.

The only disadvantage in your fur coat is that it may get tangled and matted. It is the undercoat's awn (intermediate) hairs that are most likely to mat in cats that are semi or fully long-haired. Mats may also form when your fur is being shed, as the loose hair gets caught in your coat. Yes, grooming will help stop this happening, but with long hair it is difficult for any cat to do enough grooming. Old, arthritic cats may also find it painful to swivel round to get at some areas of their fur. Fur, therefore, has its occasional disadvantages, particularly if it is long and thick if you are one of the pedigree breeds, but on the whole, it will make you more comfortable and warm than humans!

Nature and evolution have formed you well. You have a body perfectly designed for catching and eating small animals and which is also adapted to keep you safe from other, bigger predators by climbing trees. You can live, mate and have kittens in the wild all over the world often without human help. Yet nowadays you are just as likely to live inside a human home.

2

HOW YOUR ANCESTORS BECAME PETS

You are now a cat that lives in a warm house with human beings, perhaps with other cats and even a dog. Cat food is put down twice a day or maybe just left down for you to snack whenever you want. You may even sleep on the bed with your human. It is a warm, protected life in a human rather than a wild environment. Your species has adapted well to it. But how and when did you and your ancestors move into human homes?

THE FIRST FELINE

Your ancestral journey from treetops to the human household started some 30–25 million years ago with the first feline, *Proailurus*. This was the Oligocene epoch during which today's continents were beginning to drift apart, and as the temperature cooled, open plains and deserts appeared in the world and some subtropical forests were replaced by deciduous ones. This was an era when the warm-blooded mammals we know today were beginning to become recognizable predecessors of modern animals. As well as your early cat ancestor *Proailurus*, the first forms of camels, horses and canids, members of the dog family, appeared at this time. Deciding your ancestry from ancient fossil bone fragments is not an easy task and palaeontologists argue somewhat over which group of early species was your first ancestor. However, *Proailurus* seems to be the most likely candidate.

Your ancestor's fossil remains, those of *Proailurus*, were first discovered by Henri Filhol (1843–1902), a professor of comparative animal anatomy at the French National Natural History Museum in Paris, and a medical doctor by training. His photograph shows a plump, prosperous middle-aged man with a fine moustache, a bow tie, and a fob watch in his single-breasted waistcoat pocket. His life interest was palaeontology, and he published an impressive ten volumes on fossils, most of them running into several editions. The feline fossils he discovered came from the limestone outcrops and quarries of Saint-Gérand-le-Puy in France's Auvergne region, and in his opinion two of the fossils were the ancestors of today's cats. His identification was based mainly on the grounds of their teeth, as he did not have full skeletons, but just the jaw in one case.

In 1891 Filhol wrote that one of the fossil teeth 'absolutely resembles a tooth of a cat'.[1] He named the feline fossils after the Greek words for 'before' – *pro* – 'cat' – *ailuros*. It was later shown that this particular tooth did not come from what is now recognized as the *Proailurus* genus, but he had the roughly right idea, as it came from a cat-related group (*Stenogale*). In the case of the other fossil, which he named *Proailurus lemanensis*, subsequent fossil discoveries have supported his identification. *Proailurus* is the name given to a whole category of early felids (the proper word is a 'genus'[2]), which includes several different species. Of these *Proailurus lemanensis* is your likely ancestor.

What have you inherited from this ancestor down the millennia?

Proailurus lemanensis wasn't a large animal. It was only a little bigger than today's ordinary domestic cat, weighing about 9–10kg (20–22lb). In shape, with its long looping body and pointed skull, it looked rather like the modern genet or civet cat. Reconstructed drawings also give it a longer neck than today's domestic cat. Its eyes faced forwards, so that it could focus on its prey. It had a long tail, large eyes, sharp teeth and claws that were probably protractible and thus useful for climbing. Like the civets, *Proailurus lemanensis* was probably partly tree-living. Being a small animal in a difficult world, *Proailurus* may have used trees to escape predators on the ground, in the same way you and all cats still run up trees to escape dogs or other menacing animals. In a world where big animals eat smaller ones, keeping safe is a priority which, then as now, affected almost all aspects of feline lifestyle.

EVOLUTION DOWN THE AGES

As the Oligocene epoch gave way to the Miocene around 23 million years ago, *Proailurus* evolved along two pathways. We know much more about one of these pathways than the other, probably because it is more exciting and because it has a better fossil record. A descendant of *Proailurus*, *Pseudaelurus* became the ancestor of mega cats, the sabre-toothed tigers, the *Smilodon*, with their killer jaws and gigantic upper canine teeth. Who wants to research the ancestry of small modern cats when they can give their attention to rip-roaring animals like these?[3] Besides, the larger the fossil bones, the more likely they were to be noticed in the first place by people like workers in a busy quarry. Even modern palaeontologists, like ordinary folk, enjoy the thrill of the gigantic. No wonder, then, that the first fossil of a

sabre-toothed tiger or big cat was found well before anybody found
the bones of smaller cats. The palaeontologist who found it in 1842
called it *Smilodon populator* – the second half of the name meaning
'destroyer'. Again, it was the teeth that caused the most excitement –
these were thick, long upper canines ready for a spectacular killing
bite. Thousands of words have been written on how these huge
predators might have managed their long canine teeth, whether they
crunched down with the top teeth first or used the bottom jaw teeth
to move the prey into a position where the canines could pierce the
flesh. The Latin names given to these fossilized genera and species
reflected the excitement at the size of these animals and included
Dinofelis, *Smilodon fatalis* and *Amiphimachairodus giganteus*.
Perhaps humans should be relieved that these gigantic felines were
a dead end in evolution. Had they survived, they would have been
spectacular, if challenging, zoo animals, but far too dangerous to
be pets!

Your ancestral teeth were different. As a domestic cat you
descend from prehistoric cats that had 'conical' teeth, more rounded
and smaller. All the feline species alive today descend from what
palaeontologists call relatively recent history, around 11 million years
ago. In the last century, few researchers have really focused on the
fossils of these smaller cats, and far fewer fossils for these species
have been discovered. Therefore, there are big gaps in the record.
Your ancestral tree is a 'ghost' bloodline, a lineage where a series of
guesses fills in the gaps. The remains that exist are incomplete, and
it is difficult to distinguish one species from another. As a result,
the domestic cat family tree in the fossil record is difficult to work
out with certainty, though modern DNA studies have filled some of

these gaps. However, we know that an early ancestor of yours, *Felis lunensis*, was flourishing in Europe during the early Pleistocene, the time of the Ice Age. *Felis lunensis* has been called the first modern small cat. Imagined reconstructions show an animal with a somewhat longer body, longer tail and smaller head than a modern domestic cat.

WHAT'S IN A NAME?

Today your nearest extant relatives are the European wild cat and the African wild cat. Some taxonomists, the scientists responsible for sorting animals into meaningful groups, suggest that the domestic cat and these other two are subspecies, rather than separate species. As a domestic cat you are just a variation of the wild cat, so to speak. Indeed, the International Commission on Zoological Nomenclature in 2007 decided that you were no longer *Felis catus,* the domestic cat, but should now be known as *Felis silvestris catus*. This added the Latin word *silvestris*, meaning a wooded or wild area, to the cat word, *catus*. They put the wild back into your name.

And in a way this also fits in with what humans know about the lifestyle of modern cats. You can be as wild as *silvestris* or as domestic as *catus*. As a cat you are able to survive without a human owner, by poking round dustbins in a town or catching rodents among the trash. You can take advantage of human dwellings for shelter and human rubbish dumps for food, but you do not need these. You can also live as a rural feral cat, catching mice and rats, birds and insects, even on an island completely uninhabited by humans. Some experts even think that cats are only semi-domesticated, because, while many of them depend on humans for food and shelter, with the exception of registered pedigree cats, humans do not generally control their mating. This adaptability has benefited your species enormously. Indeed, the domestic cat is by far the most successful feline in the world today. *Felis silvestris catus* probably outnumbers all other felids in the world put together. Your world population is estimated at somewhere between 200 million and 600 million. The domestic dog outnumbers all other canid species today but falls short of your feline flexibility, which allows your species to transition between being wild and being domesticated. Dogs can live without human owners, but to thrive on the outskirts of human territory they often need to haunt the rubbish tips left by humans. Feral dogs are generally not found on uninhabited islands as cats are, perhaps because they could not secretly jump ship as so many ship's cats did.

As a domestic cat you are likely to have retained your instinctive wild hunting ability, although in this, as in all else, your individual behaviour will vary. In general, most cats hunt if they are given the choice, but the level of their activity will vary from cat to cat. In one study not all the domestic cats with access to a cat flap hunted regularly. The researchers studied videos from small cameras worn on the collars of 55 suburban cats for up to ten days per cat. Their hunting success varied among individuals, and only 44 per cent of these cats hunted wildlife during the short study period.[4] However, indoor-only cats, which may have never hunted a live rodent, will often learn how to hunt if they are given a cat flap later in life in rural areas. With practice they can become skilled hunters even in middle age. Many pet cats that stray from home and have to find their own food survive for several months and occasionally for years thanks to hunting rodents, delving in garbage bins, entering other cats' homes to steal food left down, or being fed by friendly humans.

Why is your species so numerous? One reason for its success is the fact that if you are female you mate whenever you have enough food and shelter to bring up kittens, and sex makes you ovulate. You are not restricted by the time of year, except in so far as a cold season or a very hot period reduces food and shelter and this restricts breeding. You breed young and (in the wild) die young. Many feral kittens will not survive their first winter, but there are always more of them in the spring. In the 1970s scientists dubbed this the r-strategy, a trade-off between quantity and quality of offspring. Your feline reproduction strategy in the wild is to mature young, breed fast and die young. The r-strategy trade-off works well for you, just as it works well for another successful species, one of your prey animals – the rabbit. You could say that cats breed like rabbits! As a female cat, you can have up to five litters a year – in theory, at least. Hypothetically, if a single female cat bred freely for five years, and if all the kittens survived and also bred in their turn, she would have 20,000 descendants.[5]

THE EFFECTS OF DOMESTICATION

Domestication, or semi-domestication, has made some changes. It has influenced not just docility around humans and type of coat, but also your coat colour. Today's domestic cats come in all sorts of colours – black and white, grey, ginger, tortoiseshell, tabby, white and black. Your direct ancestor, *Felis silvestris lybica*, the North African wildcat, is a greyish-brown animal with somewhat longer legs than its domestic cousin. Its legs are stripey, and its main body has more muted indistinct stripes. These markings and the greyish body fur are camouflage which helps it blend into the arid African bush or the Arabian Desert. (The spots and blotches found on some big cat species are better for blending into the dappled shade of a forest.) This ability to blend into the background allows wildcats to hide from predators. It also allows them to hide from their prey, as they creep up on them or sit and ambush them. As a domesticated cat you probably have lost some of this camouflage, as humans have found the unusual colours more interesting and have preferred these striking colours over others. The 'domesticated' colours of white, black and white, and ginger do not blend nearly so well into a desert background. Pedigree breeds, where humans choose which cats can mate, have become even more strikingly different in coat colour and coat length from the original cat. Even so, the changes are still modest, compared with what domestication has done to the dog. Most pedigree cats, though not all, are still shaped like an ordinary cat.

Your ancestor, the African wildcat, has been rarely studied in depth, and, indeed, in many places it may be too late to do so as it has interbred freely with domestic cats. Today's wild *Felis silvestris lybica* is likely to be partly a mongrel breed in the same way as the Scottish wildcat shows increasing amounts of domestic cat in its DNA. Identifying whether a cat is a wildcat or a domestic cat living wild merely from its outward appearance – its morphology, to use the specialist term – or from a skeleton can be quite tricky because of individual differences between animals of the same species. And till recently not much attention was paid to the smaller cats. As might be expected, the conservation of small cats attracts less research grant money than the conservation of the bigger, more spectacular felids like the snow leopard. On the other hand, the small size of smaller cat species protects them from human trophy hunters.

One of the best recent studies of your ancestor, the African wildcat, was conducted by Marna Herbst and colleagues in the Kgalagadi Transfrontier Park in the Kalahari wilderness.[6] This is open scrub savannah. These African wildcats were fitted with radio collars and tracked by a four-wheeled vehicle. The wildcats lived a solitary life, meeting up only for mating or, if female, spending time with kittens. Males had a territory which overlapped that of several different females, and the female's territory overlapped with the neighbouring female's territory. These wild cats communicated by spray marking and loud calls to advertise that they were available for mating. Softer sounds and body rubbing occurred between mother and kittens and between mating males and females. But the Marna Herbst (et al) study noted that these wildcats were 'not very vocal in general'. This account of their behaviour and lifestyle differs only slightly from the lifestyle of feral domestic cats. Interestingly, even for these wildcats, there was no distinct season for mating, though no kittens were born during a period when food was scarce. At times when prey was abundant, they could raise up to four litters a year, and this ability to breed according to food and shelter supply, rather than strictly according to season, has been carried over to you pet cats.

Adult wildcats behaved towards their kittens much as you domestic cats do, with the males giving no assistance in kitten rearing. Another fascinating finding was that, if adult wildcats encountered each other, they would stare for several minutes at a distance, then walk away to avoid an encounter. This is just what you domestic cats typically do when you meet an unfamiliar cat on the garden wall. Only dominant wildcat males would chase lesser males away. The wildcats would, of course, flee or hide from big animals such as leopards, lions, cheetahs and caracals, as these prey on them without stopping to stare! They were mainly nocturnal but flexible enough to hunt in the daylight if their prey was available. They would also tolerate being near to human settlements, unlike some small felines.

CATS AND HUMANS – AN ANCIENT HISTORY

This tolerance of humans may explain how *Felis silvestris lybica*, your ancestor, became a domestic pet. It was pre-adapted to domestication, and it was in the right place at the right time – the so-called Fertile Crescent in the Middle East about ten thousand years ago. It is here that human beings began to settle down in villages, building themselves semi-subterranean pit houses and living in them all year round. Before that, humans had been nomadic hunter gatherers, moving around the landscape according to the seasons, settling only for a few weeks or months in small tentlike shelters or caves, if there were any. This wandering lifestyle would not have suited a territorial animal like *Felis silvestris lybica*. Nor would a small wildcat be useful as an aid to the nomadic hunters, as the first dogs may have been.

However, when humans started living in one place, they became more attractive to the local wildcats. In the Fertile Crescent the humans we now call Natufians lived in such fertile surroundings that they were able settle in one place even before they started proper farming. They hunted and culled the local herds of wild animals which lived nearby, and they collected wild seeds and grains, which they stored in semi-subterranean pit houses. Once there was stored grain, there were house mice. Sparrows also moved into their settlements to feed on these food stockpiles. And where there were mice and sparrows, there was food for the local *Felis silvestris lybica*, which preyed upon them. Thus, human society provided abundant food, and the human buildings and rubbish dumps would provide some shelter, to your ancestors.[7]

The cats that moved into human territory were those individuals that were least frightened of humans, and so slowly these local cat populations began to diverge from their original wild populations. If you had been a cat ten thousand or so years ago in the Fertile Crescent, you would probably have lived side by side with humans and their dogs but without much direct contact. You might have been picked up by a Neolithic child as a kitten and sometimes taken down inside a dark little subterranean house, but you may still have been more a tamed wildcat than a domestic cat. You would still have needed to hunt for most of your food, and you would still have mated with the cat of your choice, rather than having a mate chosen by a human. You were not fully controlled by a human, as, even today, many cats are still not, but the domestication of your species was beginning.

The human–cat relationship was slowly becoming a closer one, perhaps as humans began to appreciate your pest-control abilities or were attracted by the charm of your kittens. One example of this occurred in Cyprus, where an eight-month-old cat was buried only 40cm (16in) away from a human body in the Neolithic village of Shillourokambos. This tomb is dated to about 9,500 years ago. As there is no evidence of wildcats being native to the island, it looks as if this cat must have belonged to a population of *Felis silvestris lybica* introduced by humans from the mainland.[8] The joint burial suggested that some kind of bond was likely. Of course, an animal burial in itself does not prove the cat was a loved pet: it is possible it was an animal sacrificed as an offering. Even so, this suggests the individual animal had some kind of importance, albeit perhaps just a ritual one. We cannot know for sure. There is also another, less pleasant possibility – that the cat had been buried as a sort of packed lunch for the human in the afterlife, just as other domesticated animals like sheep and cattle are kept to be eaten. In Cyprus some remains of cats with bones detached from the skeleton have been found at Neolithic sites, suggesting that humans had been eating them, tearing off the bones as modern humans might tear off a cooked chicken leg.[9] Even in modern times, such as during the Siege of Paris in 1870–71, starving humans have been known to kill and eat cats, and in some regions, for example parts of the Far East and South-east Asia, it is still culturally acceptable to eat cat.

Fast-forward from Cyprus to the predynastic period in ancient Egypt, before there were pharaohs, around 4000 BCE. Archaeologists have found another cat laid to rest in a human tomb.[10] The skeleton was that of a craftsman, buried with his tools, and at his feet were the bones of a gazelle and a cat. The gazelle was presumably for eating in the afterlife, but the cat may have been a pet, unless, of course, it was just the starter course before the gazelle, or a feline ritual offering. Once again, we cannot know for sure. During the same period was found a small burial pit containing a male cat, a female cat and four unrelated kittens belonging to two different litters. The archaeologists concerned suggested that these were domestic cats, not just desert wildcats.[11] Somewhat later, when Egypt was ruled by pharaohs, cats certainly make their mark on culture. They appear as hieroglyphs and also in nicknames. Men were called Pa-miu, or 'Tomcat', while women were Miut, Miit or Ta-miit, meaning 'Female Cat'. None of this is proof of cats living inside households, but it does suggest the possibility of a human–cat bond. Many Egyptian wall paintings remain ambiguous, as the cats portrayed outside a home setting may be wildcats or even a different wild feline species. Ancient Egyptian artists did not use perspective, and subjects could be painted large or small according to their status and whatever message the painter wished to convey. However, by around 2000 BCE the cats in tomb paintings are shown living in the house. There is, for example, a 1250 BCE wall painting in the tomb of the royal sculptor Ipuy showing him with a kitten on his lap, while there is also a cat under the chair of his wife Duammeres. The kitten has a tabby pattern, and the cat under the chair has either a tabby stripe, or even perhaps a collar, round its neck. Other tomb paintings and wall reliefs show cats under a woman's chair, too. Some are eating, some wear collars, some are there with other animals like a goose or a monkey. This context strongly suggests domestication. These are animals that have moved into the home, not just cats that are living in the yard.

CAT WORSHIP, CAT CRUELTY

If you had been a cat in ancient Egypt, you would have received a certain amount of human respect, even human worship. The Egyptians had always associated their gods with different animals. There were deities like the jackal god Anubis, a crocodile god Ammet and a lion goddess Sekmet. By 1000 BCE male cats were being associated with the sun god and the female cat was being linked with the goddess Bastet, whose cult centre was at Bubastis in the Nile Delta. The popularity of the cat cult, if we can call it this, grew when some of the pharaohs came from Bubastis and cats themselves began to have an aura of sanctity. By the 5th century BCE the Greek traveller Herodotus claimed that the death of a cat or a dog required the owner to pay their respects:

> The occupants of a house where a cat has died a natural death shave their eyebrows and no more; where a dog has died, the head and the whole body are shaven. Dead cats are taken away to sacred buildings in the town of Bubastis, where they are embalmed and buried; female dogs are buried by the townsfolk in their own towns in sacred coffins.[12]

Occasionally, archaeologists find an individual pet cat coffin. The cat Tamyt (a name meaning female cat), belonging to the son of a pharaoh, was buried in its own sarcophagus, with a carved cat portrayed on the side and an inscription which read: 'I myself am placed among the imperishable ones that are in the sky . . .'

However, human respect or even human worship given to you as an ancient Egyptian cat would not always have gone hand in hand with human kindness. By the Ptolemaic period, around the 3rd century BCE, huge numbers of cats were required as votive offerings for the cat goddess Bastet. These were specially bred in their thousands,,, then killed by strangulation or having their necks broken. Their bodies would be dried, filled with packing material like sand, then wrapped into a mummy form. Thousands were mummified and then buried in special cat cemeteries. Archaeologists have discovered at least 20 of these sites. In the 19th century when they were first discovered, about 180,000 cat mummies, weighing 20 tonnes (22 US tons), were sold at auction in Liverpool docks, to be ground up and used as fertilizer! So being a temple cat would have meant you probably led a very short life, albeit there may have been the promise of immortality.

We can assume, however, that most cats would still have led lives hunting mice in human settlements, and only some would have become valued pets living indoors. By now cats were spreading from the Fertile Crescent alongside the spread of human agriculture, fixed settlements, house mice and sparrows. Cats made their way overland and also by sea. It has been suggested that the seafaring Phoenicians may have found them useful for keeping down rodents on board, just as later seafarers did. By 411 BCE, the ancient Greek comic playwright Aristophanes (445–386 BCE) was jokingly referring to the old excuse: 'The cat did it.' Cats then reached Italy about 2,400 years ago and slowly displaced the ferrets that had been used as household pest controllers. An Italian vase in the British Museum shows two women with a cat and a pigeon. Experts estimate that domestic cats reached the British Isles about 2,100 years ago.[13] They did not reach the Americas until a mere 500 years ago and Australia until the early 1800s.

In Britain, cat bones have been found on late Iron Age and Roman sites and have been identified as domestic cat bones. However, earlier archaeologists had neither the DNA tests nor the good dating techniques used today, and identifying animal bones just by looking at or measuring them has often been subject to error. Some of these cat bones in British sites and elsewhere may have been just local wildcats. However, as Iron Age Britons traded with Rome before the Roman invasion, it seems likely that cats had arrived by traders' boats by this period. When the Romans invaded, cats came with them to their settlements as far north as Vindolanda, just south of Hadrian's Wall, where a cat skull is on view in the settlement's museum. As the wall would have been no barrier for them, no doubt some then made their way into Scotland. Then as now, you cats led lives that varied from completely wild to the household domesticated feline. Your prolific reproduction rate meant there was no barrier between the household cat and the cat that was living wild. Unowned cats mated freely with owned cats, and owned cats would sometimes leave their home or be pushed out to join their wild counterparts. Humans rarely exerted any control over feline reproduction.

A FLEXIBLE AND VARIABLE SPECIES

And that ability to adapt either to household domestication or to wild living is still in your genes. You are one of the hundreds of millions of cats in the world today that live amazingly varied cat lifestyles – thanks to the flexibility of your species. If you are one of today's feral cats, living where there is not much food around, you and your siblings spread out and lead solitary lives except for mating or rearing kittens, just like your ancestor the African wildcat. If you are female, you socialize only with your kittens or a passing tomcat. When there is enough food, often near or inside human towns where there are friendly cat feeders, you live in groups of related females with your kittens. Mothers, aunties and sisters may split the kitten-raising duties, even sharing suckling and babysitting. Males come for mating but usually move on to visit other female groups.

This sociability, however, is generally less marked than, and more variable between individuals than, the sociability of dogs. You still hunt or forage alone, rather than in a group. You still normally prefer to eat alone, only sharing food with your kittens. Outsiders are generally not welcome. You typically chase unrelated or newly arrived strays out from your territory. In many ways your behaviour has not much changed from that of your immediate ancestor, the African wildcat, and humans have not selected specifically for those more sociable features. Domestication has made some differences, mainly in the way that you can adapt to the human lifestyle if circumstances are right. Yet you remain your own cat. You are amazingly individual in your sociability towards other cats and towards humans.[14] You may be uninterested in or even scared of humans, or you may be a real cuddle cat. As for other cats to which you are not related, you may dislike or even fight with them, or you may be able to tolerate them. You may be a real loner, or you may manage to live in the house with other cats without too much conflict. You may even make a close friend of a particular unrelated cat in the house. It is possible for you to be friendly with the cat next door while hating the cat two doors up. Dogs are almost always sociable with other dogs; with cats it is much more variable. Your species has shown how adaptable it is, but you as an individual are not so flexible in your behaviour, with strong tendencies that you find hard to control.

In the next chapter we shall explore how this individuality may affect your happiness in the modern world.

3

WHAT IT IS LIKE BEING A KITTEN

Your striking individuality starts even before you are born, before you are floating in the warm bliss of amniotic fluid in your mother's womb, indeed, even before you come into being as a tiny, fertilized cell. Genes which will shape your development are switched on and off in the cells that will fuse to make the fertilized egg, according to the experience of your mother and father. Your future life is also partly shaped by the sexual encounter of your mother and father. A litter of kittens, born into an area where the cat population is high, rarely has a single father.[1] More often, there will be two or three tomcats that have mated with your mother. Of these, the tom that gives you his genes will have a major influence on your life, but the other developing kittens may affect the womb environment and so also affect your development. You may therefore have genes from your father that none of your other siblings have, even though you all share the same mother.

NATURE AND NURTURE

If your father is a friendly laid-back tom, you are more likely to grow up with a friendly laid-back temperament. If he has a nervous disposition, you are more likely to grow up to be a nervous cat. This holds good whether or not you have any contact with your father (and most kittens do not). The genes that you inherit from your feline parents will, to a certain extent, influence your future life.[2] Only to a certain extent, because, although your DNA is fixed, your genes can be switched on and off by your environment not only before birth but also during kittenhood and throughout life. Nurture is as important as nature and both co-operate to make you who you are. When you grow up with a feline mother, the way she mothers you, not just her genes, will also influence the rest of your life. Your father is usually absent, so nurturing normally comes from her and her wider social group.

If you are a pedigree kitten, the DNA you inherit may be slightly different from that of an ordinary house cat. Humans who read the descriptions of pedigree cats written by the breeders should be cautious about what they read. Yes, having a posh pedigree may affect some, but only some, of your behaviour. Scientists have compared the behaviour of Norwegian Forest kittens, for example, with the behaviour of Oriental/Siamese and Abyssinian kittens.[3] All the kittens were exposed to a frightening object: the Norwegian Forest kittens seemed to be more reactive than the other three breeds. Either these three breeds were naturally more laid back, or perhaps the Norwegian Forest kittens were slower developers. However, although DNA varies slightly between cat breeds, it varies much more among individuals within the breed than between the breeds themselves.[4] So your breed, if you are a pedigree, may shape your life a little and, of course, if you are inbred, or come from a breed with hereditary diseases, your pedigree may impact your health a lot – unfortunately for the worse. When it comes to health, your upmarket pedigree is no advantage and may even be a serious liability.

Unlike dogs, cats have been largely bred for their looks, while dog breeds were created for different functions such as guarding, herding, racing or as lapdogs. But for cats there is no inherent reason why pedigree feline behaviour, rather than looks, should differ strongly from the behaviour of a moggy. If you are a pedigree cat, you are likely to behave more or less the same way as a non-pedigree cat would. Pedigree Persians can be enthusiastic hunters, for example, if they are given the chance. Your level of sociability will vary, too, as humans rarely select for this trait, obviously preferring to raise all the kittens in a litter rather than killing off or preferentially neutering the ones that are nervous.

So, breed alone is not going to be a good guide to your behaviour in later life. Of course, if pedigree kittens are nurtured in different ways from the nurturing given to ordinary kittens, that difference too might shape your life. Your distinct individuality is largely a combination of four influences – your genetic inheritance, what happens to you before birth (prenatally), what happens to you under the care of your mother, and your early relationship with humans, other cats or other animals. Almost all animals, from ocean-living octopuses and cold-blooded tortoises to warm-blooded apes and humans, have specific individual personalities or temperaments. Cats, in particular, seem not just to have the expected temperamental range from fearful to confident but also to show very individual differences in behaviour in a human home. From the very start of your life, you and your littermates are all amazingly individual. This showed up when researchers investigated kittens' reactions in the very first month of their lives and found there were already differences even at this early age.[5]

The second stage in your development, after the genes of your father and mother have merged in the womb, happens before you are even born. The umbilical cord connects you to your mother's blood supply and therefore you share the nutrients and hormones in her blood. If your mother is a stray cat, with not enough to eat during her late pregnancy and when she is nursing you, you will be developmentally delayed.[6] There is also something else that happens to you. If your mother is given a diet that is only 80 per cent of what she needs while she is nursing, you play with little objects more often and your mother is less available to you.[7] You may be preparing yourself early for hunting because you will need to find your own food more quickly than a kitten whose mother has a better diet and therefore more milk for longer.

Your mother's condition while you are in the womb may also affect your ability to cope with stress in your life as an adult. The stress hormones that are in her blood are transported through the placenta to you. Admittedly, much of the research into this phenomenon has been done on rats (and some on guinea pigs and humans) but it has been shown that, when maternal stress hormones flood the blood supply, they can literally change the brain development of the foetus, making the offspring more stress prone.[8] It is probable this applies to cats as much as it does to rats. This makes evolutionary sense, because, if your mother lives in a stressful, frightening world, you will need to be extra cautious, not overconfident, to survive in those same circumstances. Your prenatal life prepares you for life outside the womb.

There is another way in which life before birth prepares you for the outside world, too – what kind of food you prefer. Scientists gave cat mothers a diet with one of two different flavours during their pregnancy and when nursing.[9] New-born kittens preferred the scent of the flavour their mother had been given while pregnant. At nine weeks, and even at six months of age, given a choice between a food with or without the familiar flavour, the growing kittens preferred the familiar flavour that had been eaten by their mother during pregnancy and nursing. Again, it makes sense that you should prefer the food your mother has eaten, because that means it will be safe for you to eat, too. In the wild your mother's diet of rodents, reptiles and even insects will prepare you to eat the prey that was available for her and that will also likely be available to you. Knowing what to hunt is important for a wild kitten that is going to have to catch its own food.

KITTENHOOD – THE FIRST FEW WEEKS

When you are born, you are dependent on your mother. She lies on her side so that you can nurse from her nipples. She nuzzles you, licks your backside to stimulate you to urinate and defecate, and keeps the nest clean by consuming your faeces before any parasitic worms present in them have time to mature and become infectious. She responds to your kitten cries if you are awake, hungry or fall out of the nest by calling with a 'brrp' sound, described as a trill or a chirrup. For the first four weeks, a good feline mother will spend most of her time with her kittens. Her style of mothering may influence your future life. Again, although this research into mothering has been done largely on rats, rather than cats, there is no reason to think it is not applicable to you, too. Good rat mothering produces confident offspring that are resilient in stressful situations, while poor rat mothering does the reverse.[10] These effects continue into adult life. Indeed, poor rat mothers produce female offspring that in turn become poor mothers. If you are an orphaned kitten, or have a poor mother, this may influence your coping abilities in later life. A good mother's care is what helps you to grow up to be a well-balanced adult cat in a normal world.

You also need your feline mother's colostrum – the 'first milk' that is particularly rich in bioactive substances – and milk to give you protection against diseases until your immune system matures. Early life without a mother has its difficulties. If you have been born in the wild and are unfortunate, some human may find you while you are still nursing and think you have been abandoned. They may then take you away and hand-rear you. While this is done with the best of intentions, many hand-reared kittens are probably not abandoned, and assuming you survive (many of your littermates will not), you will develop without the benefits that your mother would have provided. Commercial special cat milk can substitute for mother's milk if you are being bottle-fed by a human, but if you are being kept with your siblings but without a mother, you may start trying to nurse on them and injuring their tender skin. If you are a bottle-fed orphan kitten, you will benefit from the company of other cats – a foster feline mother, siblings, foster siblings or just friendly adult cats – to teach you how to be comfortable in a feline world.[11] If you are separated from other kittens and do not have any contact with other cats, there is a risk that you will grow up to have social difficulties with your own species. In an unpublished survey of people hand-rearing kittens, a worrying proportion of those feeding the kittens did not allow contact with other cats until after the first or second vaccination.[12]

The same unpublished survey of cat lovers who had hand-reared kittens reported that the death or sickness of the kittens' mother made hand-rearing necessary. These cat lovers used a variety of rearing methods.[13] Since there seems no generally accepted technique for hand-rearing, your future happiness as a hand-reared kitten may be reduced if your human foster parent is either poorly informed or inexperienced. Some studies of hand-rearing appear to have produced kittens that grow up to be more aggressive than expected; others report normal behaviour as an adult. Making sure a hand-reared kitten has contact with other kittens or vaccinated cats from an early age would seem to be a good idea.

The next hurdle for you in kittenhood is when you are weaned. Up till now your mother's milk has been available when you wanted it, although your mother will have had to leave the nest to get food and to eliminate. Somewhere around week four or five, if you are still in the wild, your mother will start bringing in dead prey for you, to introduce you to solid food. Around this time she begins to make her nipples less accessible to you. She will crouch rather than lie on her side with her belly exposed, or she will lie flat on her belly with the nipples below her body. Or she may spend time away from you, where you cannot reach her to suckle. If you persist too much, she may even respond aggressively. Weaning is often when you first learn to cope with frustration – that is, not having what you want when you want it. Now that your mother is no longer automatically available, you learn about coping with frustration (or not) and this ability, or lack of it, may shape your future outlook when your autonomy is restricted later in life. It is possible, but by no means certain, that the timing of events round weaning has an influence on your life. One survey suggested that if you are weaned early you may be more likely to behave in ways that are seen as problematic by a future owner.[14]

DEVELOPING YOUR SENSES

But how do you develop in your first two months after birth, before you become more independent? In the womb, you had already developed the sense of touch. It is the very first sense, and the sensations are felt by day 24 of your mother's pregnancy and about 43 days before you are born.[15] After birth, your tactile sense helps you, alongside heat sensors on the tip of your muzzle, to orient yourself to the warmth of your mother's body, as does your sense of smell, which is present from birth onwards.[16] The scent of your mother is so important to you that you will still be able to identify it a year later.[17] Scent as well as warmth is crucial for your well-being as a new-born. You cry out if you are taken away from the nest, but you stop when you are returned to it because the chemicals and odours of the nest make you feel safe. You make little sniffs and turn your head towards the odour of cat food, even though you are not old enough to eat it, showing that your sense of smell is active. You nuzzle into your mother until you find a nipple to suck on, and that nipple often becomes your nipple for about the first four weeks of nursing. When you are hungry, you find that same nipple to suck from. You do not usually have to compete with your siblings for it because they also have their own preferred nipple. You are guided to your nipple by its individual odour, a mixture of odours from yourself, your mother and the milk. When you have latched on, you will purr and tread with your front feet against your mother's body. This encourages her to let down milk. In the first days after birth, you cannot walk but you can make paddling motions with your front legs to drag yourself towards the nest, which smells of your mother, you and your siblings. The scent and warmth of the nest guide you back to it. When researchers washed away this scent, the kittens in their study found homing back to the nest more difficult. When your mother leaves the nest, as she must, your tactile sense of warmth and sense of smell help you to keep warm by guiding you to huddle into a warm group with other kittens.[18] You will also give little cries of distress if you become cold or if you are trapped under the body of your mother.

You depend strongly on scent because you are blind at birth, and your eyes are not fully open until about day 7 to day 10. Your sense of hearing is immature at birth but develops in the first few days of your life, maturing as your ear canal begins to open sometime between day 7 and day 14 of your life. Your sense of balance, the vestibular system that co-ordinates the movement of head and eyes, slowly matures from birth, so that, at the fourth week, you begin to be able to right your body in mid-air while falling. Indeed, at a month old, your sense of smell has been quite mature for the past week, your hearing is well developed, your eyes have been fully open for some time, and your vision much improved. Your ability to see clearly continues to improve for a further two or three months.

From having to paddle your legs and drag your body across the ground, you begin to develop the graceful physical motions of your species. At around day 10 you can usually stand on your own four legs, with your body off the ground. You can sit at about 20 days, and by the end of the fourth week you can walk and run and have started to learn how to climb, even if you fall off whatever you are climbing quite often! Now your claws can be retracted or extended, when for the first two weeks you couldn't protract them at all. From about three weeks onwards, you begin to urinate and defecate, without your mother having to stimulate your backside. By around 30 days you begin to take yourself to the litter tray or find a similar surface, where you rake the loose litter or dirt. You learn where to go by observing your mother and by proceeding to the latrine smell of the litter box.[19] By the time you are weaned, you have started to learn what you like and you will have formed a preference for a particular surface for urination – whether this is a particular kind of litter, loose dirt, sand or earth.

You grow fast. Your weight doubles in the first week and triples in the second week, if you suckle enough milk from your mother.[20] Your baby teeth start to fully appear from two to five weeks. Perhaps because you now have a full set of sharp little baby teeth, your mother becomes less keen on allowing you to suckle constantly. From four weeks onwards you may start to eat a little solid food, while still nursing. Your mother will influence what you eat. If you are offered a new food while she is present, you will eat it more quickly than if you are offered the same food while she is absent. Around this stage, if your mother is a feral cat, she will start bringing dead prey to you and your siblings, later bringing live prey. She will release rodents and wait for you or your siblings to pounce on them. If you do not attack them, she will kill the prey in front of you, so you see how she kills it. You learn what kind of prey you prefer to hunt from your mother, too.[21] If she brings back a rat, you are more likely to prey on rats yourself. Of course, you will hone your hunting skills with experience, becoming more skilful with practice and learning in adulthood to deal with new prey.

Your hunting movements start about two weeks from birth, when you try to bat moving objects. You perform this form of play more frequently towards the end of the weaning period, helping you to refine the eye–body co-ordination that you will need for successful hunting for food.[22] Playing with small objects, batting them around and pouncing on them is a kind of play which you often continue to do in adulthood, too, if you grow up as a pet and have humans who give you toys. This is called object play and it differs from social play with your brothers and sisters, as we shall see later. From three weeks onwards you start playing with them with an increasing number of playful moves such as pouncing, chasing, wrestling, belly-up lying, side-stepping and back arching.[23] If you are a singleton kitten, you will have only our mother to play with, but she will co-operate in your play more than she would if you had siblings. Some cats will continue to do social play with other familiar cats at relaxed moments in adulthood.

Also, from the age of about two weeks, other forms of social life, not just play, become important for your future life and happiness. You form friendships with your littermates or other kittens you have met while a kitten, which can, if you live together in adulthood, last for a lifetime. These often become your preferred friends, and you sleep with them and greet them with rubs. You also form friendships with humans – important if you are going to live in a human home, because you must learn how to be happy as a pet. This is often called the sensitive period, or sometimes the socialization period, a term which ethologists use to describe when young animals are especially sensitive to learning how to relate socially to others of their own species. If you are going to be a pet cat, this period is particularly important because you must learn to relate not just to your own species but also to an alien species, *Homo sapiens*. It is equally important if you are a feral kitten to learn how to live with other feral cats, how to hunt for your food and how to survive as a wild animal without help from humans. Many feral kittens do not survive to reach the age of six months.

YOUR SENSITIVE PHASE

Your feline sensitive period is between the age of two and eight weeks. This period describes the time during your development when your brain is maturing socially, and you are especially susceptible to learning from particular social experiences. Different animals mature at varying ages. In your case, this sensitive period kicks in when your feline senses start emerging and you are ready to be moulded by your experiences in a way that will determine your future. Very young kittens do not react with immediate fear to what is new, and it is during this relatively fearless period that you can get used to new experiences and learn to bond with different species like humans. However, fear is a protective emotion that you will later need for survival, and so you will begin to respond to threatening experiences from the age of six weeks onwards. As you get more mobile you must know how to avoid possibly harmful people, places and things – a necessary skill for surviving in a world where there are real dangers for cats. A cat (or a human) without any fear does not normally live very long.

So, the days before eight weeks are the best time to learn about the world. If you are gently handled by humans during these five or six weeks, you will grow up to see humans as part of your social life. In order to be happy and relaxed around humans you may need 30–40 minutes of daily handling, of a kind that is pleasurable for you.[24] A research programme of handling, touching, playing with a toy, and being held during this period resulted in cats that grew up to be friendlier to humans. A year later these cats were giving their human owners more emotional support.[25] Their relaxed experience with human handlers had given them the ability to be happy around humans in general. Possibly, contact with non-related adult cats, not just your mother and siblings, during the socialization period might also help you relate to and get on with other adult cats in later life, but that does not make you a gregarious socialite. Your ability to be a highly social cat probably depends on having both the right genes for this as well as the right experience.[26] So if your genes encourage you to be a loner but early experience with other cats is positive, you will get on with them, but probably still not be a fan of cat groups. Likewise, if your genes encourage sociability but you have no or bad social experiences, then your true social potential will not be revealed. It is important that your owner appreciates this, if you are expected to live with non-related cats in a household, as you may be a loner by temperament.

This sensitive period does not have a sudden cut-off at its end, and in one study the research that has led some to think about this exact number of important weeks may simply reflect that the rescue kittens were homed at eight weeks anyway.[27] You do not stop learning about the social world at the age of eight weeks; you just adapt your behaviour more slowly and focus more on other aspects of your environment. Feral kittens that have been rescued from the wild at about the age of seven or eight weeks can be socialized as household pets but will need careful human rehabilitation to prepare them to be relaxed in a human home. This is not easy and some would be better off as farm cats rather than household cats.[28] Even some adult feral cats (not previously domestic stray cats) can learn to live in a human household but only in the way that a wild robin can be tamed to take food from a human hand. It can take months or even years for an adult feral cat to overcome some of its fears. For good or ill, your early kitten years, like the early years of a child, leave a lasting impression on you which will fade only slowly, if at all.

YOUR JUVENILE PERIOD

After these first eight weeks you enter your juvenile period, which has been called the *social referencing period*.[29] This often coincides with the time that a kitten is adopted into a new household, to meet new humans, and perhaps even a family dog. If you have not had much human contact during the first eight weeks, you will be scared by this to begin with. As a well-socialized kitten you are more likely to feel at home quite quickly, but as a poorly socialized kitten, though you may bond with your new family or your owner, you are likely to remain shy of unfamiliar humans.[30] If you are a kitten that has been brought up without enough human contact in your rescue pen, you will not find your new home easy. In this social referencing period, you will have to adjust to new household smells, new noises, the TV, cars, family dogs, unfamiliar adult cats and a completely new daily routine. You will also probably have your first experience of a cat carrier. And your reaction to a new human home will be influenced by your inherited temperamental nervousness or confidence. One difficulty that may occur is that your desire to play with another kitten peaks around weeks 9 to 16.[31] If you are put into a home with a resident adult cat, that cat may react with annoyance if you pester it to play. Only if you are lucky will you find an adult cat that enjoys playing with a kitten, as some do.

Once settled, socialized to humans, and socially referenced to your new life as a pet, as a juvenile you are full of life and ready for adventure. If you have not been neutered early by a rescue shelter (more on that later), you will be beginning to feel the first stirrings of your sexuality. If you are female, you may be ready to mate at the early age of three and a half months.[32] You may not conform to the average age for fertility, which is five to nine months, because the onset of female puberty (like every other aspect of development) is not fixed by age. Maturation can be influenced by the time of year, the climate and even the presence of a fertile tomcat or an adult female on heat. Add to that the uncertainty about the exact age of rescue kittens either handed in to shelters or born outside the home to strays or ferals, and it is no wonder that unplanned pregnancy (unplanned by the human owners, that is) is common among young pet cats. Traditionally, until this century most neutered cats, both male and female, had the surgery at about six months of age. The tradition of neutering at six months, which is too late for many female kittens, may date back to the early days of veterinary care, when dogs were neutered at this age and cats were considered to be much the same as dogs.

If you are not neutered as a juvenile, or even as a kitten, the quality of your life and even your lifespan will be affected. As an un-neutered, or entire, tomcat, you will have a larger territory than females and will roam, sometimes for miles, in search of sex with a willing female. Competition between males will lead to noisy fights, bite wounds and the risk of diseases like feline immunodeficiency virus, or FIV, that are spread by saliva and blood during these fights. Even if you are born into a household, you will often become a stray when you are fully mature, if you are not neutered. You may move out of the house in search of a mate or, if you are a tom, you may be pushed out because of your smelly habit of spraying urine. If you are an unspayed female cat, you have a smaller territory and will also sometimes spray urine to advertise your sexual status. You, too, may become a stray, if you decide, as many pregnant cats do, to leave a busy household in order to find a more secluded area to make your nest and raise your kittens. You can come on heat surprisingly quickly after the kittens are born, and many feral cats become worn out by repeated kitten bearing. Life as a neutered household pet is healthier and usually lasts longer thanks to neutering and spaying.

At three months your adult teeth begin to erupt and your kitten teeth are shed. At this time, your juvenile period, if your mother is allowed out to hunt, you will follow her to learn from her example. Even if she does not hunt, the hunting instinct means that you can probably teach yourself anyway, if you are given the opportunity. Cats that do not have the chance to hunt live prey will show hunting behaviour when taught by humans to play with fishing-rod toys or when practising object play on their own. However, cats that have never learned about living prey as kittens and have to teach themselves how to hunt in later life may find the process effortful.[33] The hunting sequence of eye, stalk, pounce, grab and kill bite is instinctive, but you need experience to become more skilful and more successful.

BECOMING AN ADULT

So, when do you become fully adult? Social maturity is less easy to determine than physical maturity. However, it occurs sometime after sexual maturity, especially in males. When socially mature you may play less, spend more time hunting, develop more of a fixed routine, and slightly change your relationship with human or feline residents of the household if you are a pet. Some feline authorities say you are socially mature at the age of one to two years, while others put it at two to three years. If you are a male cat living in a feral group, you are likely to be pushed out of, or leave, the mainly female group before social maturity. If you are a pet cat, social maturity may be reached when your relationships to other adult cats in the house or neighbourhood become settled. If you were placed as a kitten in a house with one or more adult cats, when you mature you may become friendly, indifferent or even hostile towards other resident cats, and they may change their attitude towards you.[34]

Social maturity, like the other periods of a kitten's life, is a gradual process which will vary with each individual kitten and its experiences. Once your body and mind have matured and you are living a life independent of your mother, you are ready to experience a consistent umwelt – the way the world seems according to cats like you.

4

WHAT YOU SEE AND HEAR AS A CAT

Now you are no longer a kitten, let us start with how you see the world around you, and what you see in it. Sight is probably the most important way humans experience the world around them, so we begin here. Animals and humans do not see the world as it is: they see the world as they are. What they see is what they need for survival. Now you are in the cat's world, everything looks very different. What you see in front of you is not the same as that which a human sees. And your vision is not as overwhelmingly important in the daytime, compared with your other senses, as sight is in the human experience of the world. As you are looking around with your new feline eyes, you will begin to understand why vision is a less dominant sense than it is for humans. It is often thought cats have better eyesight than human beings, but you actually don't see nearly as well as a human does in the daylight hours.

THE CAT'S-EYE VIEW

Everything looks different in this cat world. A major difference is just your size, something that many cat lovers can forget. Your feline field of vision is much lower than a human's.[1] You are looking at everything from a much lower angle. Even compared with a human down on all fours, your eyeline is still a little lower than that. A human has to more or less lie on the floor to experience what a cat sees. Everything in the cat's visual world seems bigger. Much bigger. Almost ten times bigger. As you look through your new feline eyes in your new feline body, you perceive a new and strangely different world around you. Small things look big. Tiny crumbs on the kitchen floor that are almost invisible to the human eye are the size of a marshmallow to feline eyes. A field of longer unmown grass might look like an impenetrable forest. A beetle is the size of a small bun, a worm is the size of a snake, and a butterfly is the size of a crow.

The table legs tower above you like the pillars in a cathedral. The top of that same table is like the ceiling of a church hall. A kitchen chair, with its four legs, is more or less the height of a small church. The mantelpiece, eye level or a bit lower to a human, is like the parapet on a single-storey house. The living room is similar. You can see the legs of the chairs, but not the surface of the seat of the chair, which a human can see. Some of the armchairs and sofas with higher legs, the kind often found in retirement homes, have a snug little area underneath where you can hide. Other armchairs are solid right down to the carpet so there is nowhere to hide underneath, although there is always that traditional feline hiding area, the back of the sofa. In all of these the seating area is usually higher than the tips of your feline ears.

Humans walk into the living room and glance down on the armchairs and sofa; they see the seating area of a chair and decide whether to sit down on it. For you, as a cat, everything is different. You cannot see if there is a book left on the sofa seat, for instance. You have to jump up blind. You may hope that, if you back off, you may be able to see the seat surface from a greater distance. Not necessarily. Your feline eyes cannot focus as far as human eyes can. You have to be more than seven times closer to an object to see is as sharply as a human does.[2]

People often assume that cats are sharp-eyed: they are not. Humans have better eyesight. A human with cat vision would be a near-sighted person. When you as a cat look right across a big garden you cannot see the other side clearly. It is blurred to the feline eye. Humans can focus far better into the distance. You cannot. Put another way, the definition of sharp eyesight (visual acuity) in humans is 20/20 (in feet) or 6/6 (in metres) vision; the equivalent in cats is 6/45 or 20/150. That means you have to be 6m from a visual target that can be seen just as well by a human who is standing as far as 45m away – seven times further away than the cat. (Using feet and inches, a cat has to be 20ft away from a target that a human can see from a distance of 150ft.) As a cat a lot of what you see is blurred, but from afar you can still pick out important shapes, like the silhouette of another cat. That silhouette is important to you, as the angle of the tail may help you decide if the cat is friendly or not. To sum up, the furthest you can focus is about 6m (20ft) in front of you and you cannot focus on what is nearer, literally under your nose. If a cat toy is nearer to you than 25cm (10in), your focus no longer works, and it looks blurred – though you have your whiskers to help you deal with this.[3] There is more about whiskers later.

Even when you are focusing your eyes, you still will not see as sharply as humans do. What you see has blurrier edges, so much so that your visual acuity is only a little better than the legal definition of visual acuity blindness in humans.[4] Sharply detailed eyesight isn't everything, of course, even if humans do need it for reading print and for reading human faces, a particular human skill important, among other things, for assessing if another human is honest or lying. Nevertheless, you have excellent vision for your lifestyle, and it is a human-biased ignorance of the feline lifestyle to assume that your vision must always be compared to human vision. After all, as a cat you cannot read a book (and would not wish to) but equally humans cannot usually catch mice with their bare hands (and would not wish to).

True, as a cat you find it harder and slower to change the focus from near to far (or vice versa). Your feline eyes are not as good as human eyes at switching immediately from near focus to distant focus. Humans have a lens in the eye which can readily bulge and flatten; the feline lens cannot change its curvature so easily. Your eyesight is tuned to detect movement rather than static detail.

A VISION HONED FOR MOVEMENT

Dawn and twilight are what your eyes are designed for. They are particularly sensitive to movement in dim light and in the periphery of your vision.[5] If you see something moving at the side of your eyes, you will automatically start to chase it,[6] or run away from it if it looks threatening and is moving towards you. Static objects are far less likely to interest you. You will detect a scurrying tiny beetle or a fluttering wisp of dust that humans would miss. Humans may stand and stare at an unmoving painting, appreciating the smallest detail in it. Cats are unlikely to bother to scrutinize an immobile object in this way. If you are using your feline eyes to stare at a wall, it is probably because you are waiting for, or have detected, the movement of a small insect or mouse climbing up between the bricks! You also learn to ignore the static at the periphery of your vision, only noticing or waiting for movement.[7]

So, when you are sitting in front of a hole, waiting to ambush the mouse when it comes out, you will wait for hours. That is being a cat. You will be staring, intent on detecting if there is the smallest movement of a mouse on its way out into the open. That is what interests you, not the size or structure of the hole itself. The importance of movement to you, as a cat, is best seen when you are playing with a dead mouse. When the corpse is still, you lose interest in it, so you poke it with your paw to move it. Then the game begins again, and you will be able to see it better and play pounce more accurately. As long as it is moving, you are interested and the game can continue.

How much can your eyes see? The width of what can be seen, side to side, is called the *visual field*, and yours is somewhat wider than a human's, although like human eyes your eyes are set in the front of your head. You see 200 degrees side to side, while a human sees 180 degrees. That means that you can see the horizon a little wider left to right than a human can.[8] Of your 200 degrees of visual field, 140 degrees are binocular – that is, both eyes can focus together in this area, giving better three-dimensional vision. That depth of vision allows you to focus on and pounce on small animals that are moving.

In contrast, prey animals, vulnerable to being hunted, have eyes set at the side of the head. Horses, for instance, have a much wider field of vision at 350 degrees thanks to eyes at the side, allowing them to check for enemies on the horizon much further away – not just in front but at the side also, with only a small blind spot right behind them. The range where both of their eyes can focus is much smaller than yours at only 65 degrees. This binocular area may help them browse the leaves of shrubs or trees, but field of vision is more valuable than judging distances if you are a horse. Your feline visual field is a compromise between your predatory need to focus on and thus catch small animals and your need to keep a bit of an eye out for approaching bigger animals that might catch you. For close-up judgement, you have whiskers.

THE FELINE WORLD OF COLOUR

As a cat, some of the colour has drained out of your feline world. But this does not make it a black-and-white world. Two university researchers trained cats to distinguish colours using tuna-fish rewards.[9] The cats had to distinguish various different-coloured lights from a colourless white light to get the reward. When the cats were trained in this rewarding way, they behaved as if they only saw two colours, just as dogs do. However, it seems cats have the three pigments in their eyes needed to see a similar range of colours to humans (what is known as *trichromatic vision*). Professor Ron Ofri, co-author of *Slatter's Fundamentals of Veterinary Ophthalmology*, explains:

> Behavioral studies have failed to demonstrate trichromatic vision in cats. However, quite a few studies demonstrate that cats have the anatomical basis for trichromatic vision. In other words, they have the potential for such vision, but don't use it. It's like having a 4x4 car, but never engaging the 4-wheel drive and using only 2x4.[10]

Cats have the capacity for trichromatic vision but do not use it in experiments like the one described here – another mysterious aspect of life in the cat's world!

As you look around your human home, the carpets, the soft furniture and the curtains, chosen by your human for their wide colour mix, are now less distinctive. And you may not pay any attention to them. Why should you? Although you can see many colours, colours have little meaning. You don't eat fruit, so you don't need to know if that banana on the kitchen table is an unripe green or a ripe yellow. You do not need colour to hunt. You need motion-sensitive vision and acute hearing and smell. You have far fewer colour-sensing cells (called *cones*) in your eyes than fruit-eating humans do. Humans have 199,000 cones per square millimetre, while cats have a mere 27,000, and so you cannot produce high-resolution colour images because the cones are less densely packed in to central area of the retina.[11] Cones are important because they provide high-resolution colour sight in daylight and their outer segments contain the molecules that absorb the three primary colours of red, green and blue. But who needs strong colour vision to hunt a mouse? You are hunting in dim light anyway. A mouse is a mouse, whether it is a white pet mouse or an agouti-coloured wild mouse. The smell and shape, not the colour, tell you it is a mouse and therefore edible. Nor is the colour of cat toys important to you. Your human may choose a brightly coloured soft toy mouse, but you will not care. And when well-meaning humans leave cat toys lying around in the living room, you won't be very interested in these static items. Only if they move or wiggle, or you paw at them to make them move, will they get your attention.

NIGHT AND TWILIGHT

Your night vision is much better than a human's. Moonlight is your world, and you come into your own when dusk falls and the stars come out. At the point when a human cannot see anything because of the lack of light, you can still see and continue to see till it is about six times darker.[12] You see in the dark with an amazing accuracy and a clarity which would be envied by any human. Total darkness might stop you seeing, but few places in the modern feline world are totally dark. There are not just the moon and stars in the night sky but nowadays there are car lights nearby or, at a distance, streetlights and lit-up windows, and the sky itself reflects back the lights of any big town. However, moving from a lit living room into this twilight world may mean you are blinded while your eyes adapt and thus you are at most risk then. The darkness of low light, of dawn approaching, or of the day fading into twilight are your preferred times. The dim-light darkness is when wildlife emerges – rabbits come out of their burrows to graze the cornfields and rodents venture out of their holes to look for food.

This is when you see most clearly. The large size of your feline eyes in your small face lets in every little bit of light. In the human head the eyes are relatively smaller than the face in surface area. Size matters when the eye is straining to capture every detail in low light. The diameter of a cat's cornea, the outward surface of the eye, and the diameter of the feline's eye pupil are much larger than the equivalent in humans. It has been reported that the surface size of the cornea in a human is $95.3mm^2$, while the surface of a cat's cornea is $206mm^2$.[13] That's roughly twice the size. There is an even bigger difference in pupil size. A fully dilated human pupil is 28.3mm^2 compared to 78.5mm^2 – approximately two and a half times the size.[14] About five times more light can enter the feline eye than can enter the human eye.[15] Fortunately for you, in bright light you can reduce both the size of the pupil into a vertical slit and the visible surface size of your eye with your eyelids. You even have a third eyelid called the *nictitating membrane* which acts as protection for the eye. It emerges from the corner of the eye and removes debris from the surface when needed.

As a cat you need to see in the dark. You are designed by nature to kill in twilight, during moonlit nights or during the low light of dawn when the prey is most active. To help you hunt (even though nowadays you spend more time lounging on the sofa), you have about three times as many low-light perceiving cells (called *rods*) per millimetre in your eyes than humans do.[16] There are 160,000 rods per square millimetre in a human eye compared with 460,000 per square millimetre in a cat eye.[17] The rods help you see very well in poor light. The downside is that they do not allow you to see in colour. But, after all, colour is not important in a twilight world. Even humans cannot see colours in the dark, because cone cells, sensitive to colour, are not responsive at low light levels.

Your glow-in-the-dark feline eyes have always intrigued humans. Seven hundred years ago, a medieval monk writing an early encyclopaedia marvelled that a cat 'seeth so sharply that he overcometh darkness of the night by shining of the light of his eyen'.[18] The reason for these shining eyes is that as a cat you have a reflective layer like a mirror (called the *tapetum lucidum*) at the back of your eye, which throws back the light on to your retina (the innermost photosensitive layer of the eye) to maximize any light. This is why your eyes flash iridescent in moonlight or in the headlights of a car. But the tapetum, by throwing the light back on to the retina, has a drawback. It means your sight is even less sharp, yet another reason why your vision is more blurry than human sight. This is the price of excellent night vision.

Because you are a twilight hunter, you have eyes that may need to block out too much bright light. The iris in your eye (the coloured part) can react automatically and immediately to light, with a local reflex that can bypass the brain and so respond more quickly to changing light levels – an adaptation to living in this twilight world of changing brightness, where a flash of light might otherwise temporarily blind you, as your sensitive cells are bleached out and take time to recover.[19]

People have wondered if cats can see ultraviolet (UV) light as birds do. The lenses of your feline eyes probably do admit UV light; this is common among nocturnal animals.[20] However, the UV rays transmitted through the lens may not register in the brain. Professor Ron Ofri explains: 'UV light may be transmitted through the ocular tissue and reach the feline retina. But the retina does not have the proper pigment to absorb light at the UV wavelength. So it is not actually seen.'[21] If you could see it, the UV light would be useful for tracking, because rodent urine contains a UV pigment.

THE FLICKER FACTOR

There is another way your feline vision differs from human vision. It is the flicker factor, which allows you to see things as continuous movement. Humans can only detect about 45 separate images or flashes per second before they blur into one continuous moving image, while cats can detect as separate images up to about 70 per second.[22] Fluorescent lights flicker very fast all the time but usually too fast for humans to see the flicker, so to humans the flickering fuses into a continuous light (although some people can detect the flicker around this threshold and develop headaches in this light after a while). As a cat, you can detect that fast flicker, and the flickering of fluorescent lighting may be unpleasant for you. There is no reason to believe that cats cannot also suffer from headaches. The same goes for old-fashioned television sets, which have a lower flicker rate than high-definition ones. You, a cat, see a flickering screen, rather than the clear picture seen by a human. Newer, high-definition TVs, with their higher-frequency flicker, are more likely to be seen by you as a continuous picture.

So why do some cats, especially young kittens, get interested in what is happening on the screen? Why do you, as a cat, occasionally go back behind the TV set to see what you can find there? That may sometimes be because of what you hear from the TV, rather than what you see on the screen. Or the smooth-flowing image seen by humans, perceived by you as a jumpy moving image, may be of interest to you anyway. If it is the sound from the TV which interests you, you then use your eyes to see it or move to a place where your eyes might be able to see it hiding behind the TV.

THE ACUTEST SENSE – HEARING

Your ears guide your eyes. As a cat you have supremely good hearing. Your feline world is full of tiny, almost imperceptible noises, high-pitched little cries, innumerable insect murmurs and ultrasonic rodent squeaks and laughter (yes, rats laugh!). You will hear the squeal of a mouse, the cry of a bat flying by, the rustling of a vole moving in the grass, and the rasp of an insect wing, as well as the deep barking of a big dog. Humans can just about hear the cry of a bat at twilight when they are young, while their hearing is still acute. Scientists call the high-frequency sound of a bat's cry an *ultrasonic* noise, and, as humans age and go slightly deaf, they can no longer hear it. A bat's cry is as clear to you as a cat as the ringtone of a phone is to its human owner.

For you, moving in the feline world of ultrasonic noises, which can be pitched two or three times higher than most humans can hear, these are everyday noises. How? Because you have possibly the broadest range of hearing found in any mammal that has been tested.[23] That means you can hear very, very high-pitched sounds, as well as quite low-pitched ones. In all, your hearing range, from low to high sounds, is 10.5 octaves. The human range of sound is only 9.3 octaves. Scientists measure the pitch of sounds from their wavelengths. In low-frequency sounds the wavelengths are long, and in high-frequency sounds the wavelengths are short. The measuring unit is a hertz (Hz), which is one wave per second: kilohertz (kHz) are one thousand cycles per second. The human range of hearing is about 20Hz to 20kHz.

Your feline range starts at the relatively low-frequency sound of 48Hz and reaches into high-pitched ultrasonic sound of 85kHz, which is completely inaudible to the human ear.[24] A bat's chirp at, say, 45kHz is easily heard by you. Even the ultrasonic noises of tiny insects are detected by your ears. Hearing these high-pitched sounds is not that unusual among smaller animals. However, most animals that can hear that high cannot hear the low-pitched sounds that you can hear. Your ability to hear relatively low sounds is what might be expected from an animal of your size, and therefore, if cats were like most other animals, your top limit for audible high-pitched sounds would be only around 46.5kHz.[25] Unusually, you have developed the capacity to hear much higher sounds without losing the ability to hear the relatively low ones.

Evolution has selected the ability to hear ultrasonic sound in cats, because you prey on small rodents. If a nest of mice is hidden in the grass, you cannot see it but you can hear the tiny high-pitched squeaks of the mice inside – an example of how feline hearing can guide feline eyes to search out prey. It is obvious, therefore, why you need to hear very high-pitched sounds, but it is less obvious why you have retained, rather than lost, the ability to hear relatively low sounds. However, could this ability to hear lower sounds have been retained because of your need to escape larger predators – for example, the need to hear the relatively low sound of a predator like a dog whose growl is between 80 and 300Hz?[26] If so, your feline wide range of hearing reflects your dual nature as a cat – both prey and predator.

DETECTING DIRECTION

Mammals have two ears that allow them to focus on a sound and know where it is coming from. The sound will reach the ear nearer to it earlier than the ear further away and in the same way will be louder in the nearer ear than in the further-away ear. Ultrasound with its short wavelength is easily absorbed, and so the amount of ultrasound also differs between the ears according to the direction of source. You make use of all of these indications – time, noise intensity and differences in the composition of the various frequencies – to help you locate the area from which the sound is coming. One group of scientists who tested the feline ability to locate sounds did this by tracking cat eye gaze (not allowing head turns) towards the direction of a sound. They reported that the ability to get the exact location from a sound alone was not quite as accurate as when the cats were locating a visual target. The cats also found it more difficult to work out where a short sound was coming from, compared to a longer sound.[27] Unsurprisingly, since cats are very individual in all sorts of ways, the cats varied in their individual ability and what the researchers called their *motivational level*.

Different animal species vary widely in their ability to locate where sounds are coming from. Your ears help detect if a sound is in front of you or behind you, because the sound is louder at the open entrance to the ear and fainter when it has to travel through the back of the ear. This works even in immobile human ears. Your feline ears can swivel so that they point forwards, sideways or backwards, and can lower themselves to the side of the head. This mobility helps you channel the sound to the ear and is useful for communication, too – more on that later. Even so, compared with human hearing with immobile ears, animals with mobile ears are not always as good in finding out the exact direction of a sound as might be expected, because in small mammals swivelling an ear only helps with the detection of high-pitched sounds, not low-pitched ones.[28] Evolution has produced the best sound-localization ability among those animals with a small field of accurate vision, like cats and humans. Keen hearing goes with narrow eye focus because good sound localization is needed to guide that narrow focus, and help the eyes move to where the ears have located the sound.[29] Therefore, humans, whose vision is sharper and with a smaller area of focus than that of cats, are also superior in their ability to detect the whereabouts of a sound.

All animals respond to a sound better if it is one that matters to them. Researchers call this *biological significance*. Your world, like the world of humans, is full of sounds, and you need to tune out those that are irrelevant, in order to focus on the ones that your survival depends upon.[30] As a cat, you will be primed to notice and attend to the squeaks of small mammals and the high chirps of birds, and you will tune out irrelevant noises. Experience will help you decide what can be tuned out. Take the sound of a TV set as an example. When you were a kitten or a young cat, you were more likely to go behind the TV set to look for birds or mice making noises on wildlife programmes. As you age, you learn that the sounds from the TV are not of interest to you. There is nothing interesting behind the set! Like most cats, you just ignore them, while humans, for whom TV is important, pay attention to them.

As a cat you can also hear noises that are very faint to, or below the volume threshold for, humans. The loudness or intensity of any sound is measured in decibels (dB). You are approximately as sensitive to the loudness of low-pitched sounds as a human is, but for higher-pitched sounds feline hearing is far more sensitive and you hear what the human ear cannot.[31] If there is a mouse nest behind the skirting board, you can hear the mouse pups squeaking. It is outside the range of humans in terms of pitch but also potentially too quiet for them. By contrast, a rat tiptoeing along the beams of an attic will be in the pitch range of a human but not loud enough for a human to hear. However, you will hear it. When you sit by a hedge you are not just using your eyes; you are also listening for the slightest squeak or rustle of a mouse that your eyes cannot see. You can detect a faint noise in the hedge that a human could not hear at all. Being able to hear these tiny sounds is a great help in your ambush style of hunting.

SENSE AND SENSITIVITY

This ability is not always helpful in your domestic life. You can hear noises in the home that human beings cannot. You can hear the faint high buzz of a smoke detector that is failing, or the small high click of a slow cooker turning on and off. When the washing machine is active, you hear much more than a human does, especially when it spins fast. This is potentially scary! You can hear high-pitched sounds of clicking, buzzing, whirring and grinding as a device heats up, cools down or stops – sounds additional to the sounds that humans hear. When electrical devices heat up, it is not just the smell that may upset you; it may also be a faint high buzz that humans cannot detect. And many noises that are quiet to a human ear will sound much louder in your sensitive ears. Some of the higher sounds coming out of phones or TV sets may also be distressing for you, particularly if you are a cat of a nervous temperament.

Sometimes these noises cause problems in the cat–human relationship. Humans who put the litter tray in the utility room never think that the sound of the washing machine nearby may be disturbing. What cat wants to use a litter tray if there are high-pitched whistling, grinding and clicking noises nearby, as well as the ordinary sounds that humans hear? Where is the necessary privacy if the drying machine is buzzing or wheezing in a way that screams in your ears, though not in those of humans? Humans rarely think of that. Nor do they think when they purchase an ultrasonic rodent deterrent. Yes, it may deter mice and rats with its ultrasonic screeching, but it can also badly upset cats with their sensitive hearing.

To sum up, the problem for you as a pet cat is not that you see and hear differently from a human. The problem is that humans do not always appreciate this.

5

WHAT YOU SMELL, TASTE AND TOUCH AS A CAT

You smell, taste and touch the world differently from a human. Scent, in particular, is important to you. Your world, your umwelt, is as much a smellscape as a landscape. A smell can tell you important things like 'This is the privet bush where I found a mouse last week' or 'This is the cupboard with the cat treats inside it and it smells as if the door might be half open.' Every significant thing in your home or territory has a smell that identifies it to you. There is the familiar smell of your loving human (an identifying individual scent) and also the unfamiliar smell of the workman who is servicing the boiler. The kitchen floor smells of your paw pads, your human's shoes, the lingering smell of the familiar cleaning fluid used a few days ago, and, if you are lucky, the delicious new smell of a food fragment that fell out of a sandwich a few minutes ago!

THE FELINE SMELLSCAPE

You note any changes in the familiar scents around your environment. Small changes of scent that remain unperceived by humans are noted and assessed by you. The family dog comes home smelling slightly different when he has been at the grooming parlour, because they have shampooed him. When your human comes back from work, you can smell on her either the familiar scent of her office or the medical smell of the hospital where she has had an appointment. This hospital smell, which is not unlike the smell of a vet's surgery, may worry you. You will notice any change of scent around the litter tray – a new type of litter with a different scent, a new litter tray smelling of new plastic, or a new cleaning fluid that has been used on the tray. If your soft cat bed is cleaned in the washing machine, you will note that it has lost its familiar scent. You will also notice any change in the overall smell of the household. For you there is a family scent mixture that is made up of your own scent, all the individual humans' scents, and the scents of all other pets. This is the reassuring signature scent of your safe territory. It says 'Home'.

This feline experience of scent is a world that is still a mystery to humans. Smells do not feature much in the thinking life of most humans, but they feature large in your feline world. Humans have a good sense of smell, but they do not pay much attention to it or use it much in normal circumstances. A smell may be evident to a human's nose, but they often tune it out. For example, humans get so used to the smell of traffic fumes as they walk down a street that they probably are not consciously aware of them much of the time. They can smell the car fumes and they would notice them if someone drew their attention to them, but because humans expect these fumes in city streets, they will probably pay no heed to them, unless the fumes are unusually powerful. The smellscape of either a human or a cat is not just about the nose's efficiency; it is even more about what the brain registers from the nose.

So, whether human or cat, the world of scent is not just how well we can physically smell, but what scents are relevant to us and what gets our attention so that we do smell it. One example is the smell of mice. The human Celia had two pet white mice that lived in an aquarium when she was a child. They were smelly, and visitors would notice this. But Celia got so used to their scent that she stopped noticing it at all. The family cats, however, would react with amazingly strong interest to the smell on her hands after she had handled them, sniffing carefully and thoroughly. For them, because they were mouse hunters, the smell of the mice on her hands was very important; for Celia, the smell was just a by-product of cleaning the aquarium and of no great interest. Like Celia's cat, you will be intensely interested in the smell of any rodents. You may, for instance, detect the faint smell of a mouse that has made its nest behind the skirting board, even though your humans are not aware of this. Mouse smells must be strong before humans even notice them!

Why should scent be more important to you as a cat than to us as humans? Probably because you need to use your sense of smell more often than humans do and in different ways. You cannot read or use words as humans do, and most importantly you cannot leave a long-distance message by writing or emailing. So some of the information you and other cats need to communicate comes to or from you via odours. You use scent to leave a message for other cats. They use scent to leave a message for you.

You also need your sense of smell for hunting because it is your sense of smell together with your excellent hearing that will help you detect a small rodent hidden in the grass. From the scent it has left you will be able to detect where it put down its feet, just as a bloodhound can detect a human from the scent of footprints. In the dark, even though you see better at night than humans do, that feline sense of smell will also help you find your way around. You cannot use car headlights or a torch to recognize where you are going, as humans do, but landmarks may have a particular kind of smell, or you may have marked parts of your territory so that you can recognize significant places in the dark. (There is more about this later.)

Finally, for an animal that likes to keep a distance between itself and other cats, your sense of smell will help you identify friendly, non-friendly or completely strange cats from their scent without having to get too close. Every cat and indeed every human has an individual body scent, a signature mixture of individual odours.[1] This signature scent is an important way that cats identify friends and foes. This identifying scent is more important to you than to a human. And, finally, scent is a very important tool for feline communication, while conscious deliberate scent communication between most humans is often confined to putting on perfume or aftershave to attract potential partners!

NOSE TO THE GROUND

Your feline world of scent is different from that of the human world in other ways, too. A simple difference is that most of what you smell is odours low down in the air. Why? Because your nose is lower down than a human nose, near the grass, near the carpet, at the same level as the skirting boards of a room, close to the fresh earth of a seedbed, or the bottom of the lamp post where a dog has urinated. Yet again, the simple fact of being a different size, nearer the ground, influences what molecules of scent are inhaled into your nose and what particular scents will be of interest to you. It is a rich world of scents that humans sometimes cannot smell (because their noses are so much higher up) or do not bother to smell. Occasionally, a human may kneel down on all fours to sniff at a carpet, when something has been spilled upon it. Yes, they can smell the carpet if they lower themselves, but the scent they smell may well have a different meaning in their minds from the meaning the odour has for you.

It is also important to note that with scent, as with vision, the fact that you can detect something does not mean you use that information, and cats are very individual in how they sense their world. In one study with a small number of cats, trained to use a maze, some of them used a visual cue to help them reach their goal, but one cat consistently relied on a scent cue. You may be a cat that prioritizes sight over scent, as most humans do, or a cat that prioritizes scent over sight.[2] If you are a cat that relies more on scent than on sight, your individual behaviour will differ from that of a cat who is more sight orientated. This extra importance of scent in your individual world may make it harder for your human to understand why you are behaving the way you do.

Comparisons between your world and the human world of scent are difficult for humans to fully grasp. Geneticists have now identified the genes that code for scenting abilities, the odour-receiving receptors on cells in the noses of animals, including humans. Comparing the number of genes for different species, it turns out that humans and other primates such as chimpanzees and macaques have fewer functioning genes for odour-receiving receptors compared with, for example, dogs.[3] It has been suggested that as humans need to use eyesight more than smell for their lifestyle, some of their odour genes have been lost or have become non-functioning. Professor Matthias Laska of Linköping University in Sweden, a world authority on smell sensitivity in different animals, notes: 'There is no published paper yet which ever reported on olfactory performance in domestic cats. Accordingly, it is impossible to make any comparisons between the cat's sense of smell and that of other species.'[4] Your sense of smell, therefore, and its ability to distinguish different smells or pick up very faint traces of scent, remain an unknown world to humans.

Real problems face an odour researcher trying to examine the sensitivity of an animal's nose. Researchers testing cats face more difficulties than most. Dogs have been trained to put their head into a fMRI (functional magnetic resonance imagery) scanner and stay still while researchers examine what parts of the brain are activated by different smells. While you and other cats could perhaps be trained to do this, it would take many long hours of very expert training or perhaps very heavy sedation. Another problem is the individuality among humans and cats in how sensitive they are to smells in general and to individual aromas. Professional wine-tasting human beings, for example, can differentiate with extreme accuracy the various flavours of wine, which normal drinkers usually cannot. As well as having an innately good sense of smell, they have practised and taught themselves how to distinguish the different odours and flavours in wine. They have learned to pay attention to small odour differences. They have trained not just their sense of smell but their brain's ability to make distinctions and judgements about odours. You could probably be trained in a similar way to detect odours, as are sniffer or medical detection dogs today.

But your anxiety outside your familiar territory prevents you and most other cats being useful in these roles.

It is also very important which smells are tested on which species. Each species will have odours that are particularly important to them. While a human keeping mice can become relatively immune to the smell of their pets, only noticing the whiff if they have forgotten to clean them out, the smell of a small rodent has a particular significance to cats. It rouses their hunting instinct with the promise of a fresh meal. So, comparisons between humans and cats using the smell of a mouse would not be fair to the human. Testing with a different odour, perhaps the smell of a fruit salad, a dish many humans enjoy, a human might well perform better than you do. You do not need to smell a fruit odour as you do not eat fruit. Comparisons between your scenting ability and that of a human are not a simple matter, nor are they very useful.

Both individual humans and cats vary in their smelling ability and in what odours get their attention. There seem to be smells that turn some cats on. The best known of these are catnip, the *Actinidia kolomikta* vine and valerian. Even so, not all cats get high on these plant odours, and you may be one of those cats that is just not interested. And there are some odd smells that get just a few eccentric cats excited – olives, fresh pears (sniffed but never eaten), Olbas Oil, Vicks VapoRub, Deep Heat pain-relief spray and even wet swimwear.[5] If you are one of these cats, your world of scent may be individually different from other cats' worlds of scent.

HOW GOOD IS A CAT'S SENSE OF SMELL?

The anatomy of the feline nose has prompted some authorities to suggest that your feline capacity to distinguish very faint scents and to differentiate between thousands of odours might be as good as a dog's.[6] The template for the structure of a nose is approximately the same in all mammals – two nostrils that detect the scent as air is inhaled during breathing. Having two nostrils, rather than a single nostril, allows the nose to focus on where the scent comes from in the same way that two ears allow the location of sound. Anatomically, the feline and the canine nose are not that different. Inside at the back of your feline nose is a highly folded membrane covered with protective mucus below which are special cells that receive odour molecules. From here the cells transmit a message to the main olfactory bulb in the brain, which then relays the information to other brain structures. Despite cats being smaller than humans, the nose membrane is up to ten times larger than a human one – $20cm^2$ compared with $2-4cm^2$ in humans.

The general view is that, because of anatomical differences, cats must have a sense of smell that is better than humans'. It has been claimed, and the claim can be found on many websites, that a cat's sense of smell is 14 times better than that of a human, though not quite as good as a dog's. Dogs have up to 300 million scent-receiving cells in their noses, and the claim has been made that they are therefore 40 times better at scent detection than humans. The problem with these claims is that nasal anatomy, on its own, is no guide to scenting ability. Being able to detect something is not the same as routinely using it. Professor Matthias Laska, the sensory physiologist, is clear on this point:

More than a hundred years ago, comparative anatomists put forward the notion that the size of neuroanatomical features should be predictive of an animal's sensory capabilities. Today, we know that this is not the case. Neuroanatomical features do not allow us to reliably predict the olfactory capabilities of a species.[7]

All that can be said with certainty is that your feline behaviour suggests that scent is a very important aspect of your world, and you use your sense of smell more often than humans do and in different ways.[8]

Besides, you have something that humans generally lack – a second chemical detection organ in the nose, which has a separate pathway to the brain, going directly to areas that control emotional arousal, beginning with the accessory olfactory bulb. This is the *vomeronasal organ*, also called *Jacobson's organ*. (This exists in humans in a vestigial and largely non-functioning form.) Your genes include 28 associated with one kind of vomeronasal receptor, compared with only 9 for dogs.[9] Mice, incidentally, have more than eight times as many of these genes as you do, and more than 26 times as many as do dogs. However, it would be unwise to assume that this by itself proves feline superiority over dogs in chemical detection ability within the vomeronasal organ.

The two entrances to the vomeronasal organ are inside your mouth, just above your front teeth. Ordinary scents reach the nostrils as air is inhaled either in ordinary breathing or deliberately sniffed in. Air containing novel odours or certain key scents (e.g. urine) is pumped into your vomeronasal organ by sucking, not sniffing. To do this, you open your mouth, open the vomeronasal slits in your upper mouth, and curl your upper lip to suck them in. It looks as if you are gaping or grimacing, and this is called the *flehmen response* (from the German for 'to bare the upper teeth'). This can activate particular emotions associated with these odours, if the right molecules (pheromones) are present amid these odours.[10]

Feline pheromones are scent molecules to which humans are generally nose blind. They are specialist chemical signals, sometimes called *social odours*, specific to your species, produced and received only by you and other cats. They are a kind of instinctive cat-to-cat odour language. The best-known pheromones are those that cause sexual arousal in many species, but there is a growing science around other forms of emotional arousal caused by different pheromones – some are exciting, some are calming. You do not have to learn to recognize these chemicals or the associated responses in the way that you learn the particular signature smell of the next-door cat and how to greet him or her in the best way. Your response to pheromones is innate rather than acquired through experience.

There are several different feline pheromones, and they are complex mixtures of chemicals rather than a single odour molecule. One example is the pheromone given off by a nursing mother cat from the scent glands round her nipples: the kittens, even before they can see or hear, can detect this pheromone. It helps the mother and babies feel secure and relaxed with one another. Together with the ordinary scent of the mother's belly and her body warmth, it signals to the tiny, blind and deaf kittens that their mother is a source of security. The pheromone also means the maternal nest is a safe place, and so they will start crying if they fall out or wander away by accident. Other pheromones come from the chin region and also provide reassurance, which is why you rub against things to increase their familiarity. Feline reactions to pheromones have been used to make artificial sprays and plug-ins to help cats like you feel emotionally secure, now that humans know a bit more about them.

THE FELINE SMELLSCAPE

For both cats and humans, the sense of smell makes an enormous contribution to the sense of flavour. You, like humans, use your sense of smell when you decide whether to eat an unfamiliar food. The smell of fresh food, rather than the odour of a decaying corpse, is important to you because you are not a scavenger. A dog will eat meat that is going off; you will not, unless you are starving. You sniff unfamiliar food before tasting. The sensation of taste then checks in as soon as you start eating it, even though you swallow your food quickly rather than chew. Because you have a vomeronasal organ, which opens into the mouth, the aroma of the food, as well as its taste, is also emotionally important to you while you are eating it. You are likely to go off your food if your sense of smell has disappeared due to a respiratory infection, as both taste and smell are important for you to enjoy the full flavour of the food.

The world itself tastes different to you now that you are a cat. Taste, like smell, is part of your umwelt. 'Each animal lives in its own sensory world that is coordinated with its diet,' according to Dr Gary Beauchamp, a well-known researcher into taste, smell and flavour at the Monell Chemical Senses Center, Philadelphia.[11] Not just warm-blooded animals but even fish have taste buds. It is important for any animal's survival to choose food that is safe, not poisonous, and to choose food that is nutritious. Taste helps an animal to seek out the right food for its needs. As a cat you may taste as intensely as a human does, but you taste fewer and different flavours than those tasted by humans. You only have about 475 taste buds, on the tip and sides of your tongue and elsewhere in the mouth. Each taste bud is a cluster of cells with sensing fibres, located at the surface of the tongue. These receive taste sensations and send a message to the brain. This is a very small number compared with humans, who have 9,000 taste buds, and dogs, which have about 1,700.[12] Your taste buds, just like your teeth and gut, are adapted to being a strict carnivore, eating meat, not vegetables or fruit. You do not need to experience some of the taste sensations necessary to animals that eat a more varied diet. Both humans and dogs eat a mixed diet of plants and meats, so they need to know whether a berry is ripe and therefore safe to eat, as much as if the food is rotten. This does not matter to a cat, whose meals in the wild consist only of other animals – thus, you have fewer taste receptors and fewer taste buds gathering them together.

One of the five main human tastes – sweet, sour (acid), salty, bitter and umami (the meaty savoury flavour) – is missing in your life. You cannot taste sweetness. The gene that in humans and dogs functions for this taste is switched off in you.[13] So why might you enjoy licking ice cream offered by a human? It is not because it is sweet. It is because ice cream contains fat, and that is what your taste buds are responding to. You are also not as sensitive to saltiness as some animals are, probably because the salty sodium you need would normally be found in the bodies of your prey and so you are unlikely to ever go short, so long as you are eating your natural diet.[14] Some authorities, rather surprisingly, suggest that your taste buds are designed to select safe versus harmful tastes, rather than enjoyable versus unpleasant tastes.[15] However, it is more likely that your taste buds combine both functions. You certainly show signs of enjoying or disliking the food presented to you.

The need for a strict carnivorous diet does not stop your feline taste buds being able to taste the bitter flavour. A look at your genetic make-up suggests that the genes for tasting bitter are functioning fine, unlike the gene for tasting sweetness.[16] No wonder you spit out many of the pills that humans may try to put down you. You can taste their horrible bitter flavour. Your taste buds can also taste the umami meaty flavour well, and it is very attractive to you in your food. Indeed, you may taste more flavours in meat than humans do! This sensitivity to meaty flavour is what is thought to drive your food preferences.[17] As cat-loving humans know only too well, many cats show a preference for the higher-priced cat foods, probably because these usually contain a greater proportion of the more expensive meat ingredients.

In addition, there are some other commonly accepted tastes, *secondary tastes*, that humans can taste, and you probably can, too. These include the metallic taste, the fat taste, astringency (the taste that makes the mouth pucker) and the kokumi taste. (Kokumi, confusingly, doesn't actually have a specific flavour; instead, it is a kind of flavour enhancer.) The kokumi flavour is more important to you and other carnivores than it is for humans.[18] It seems to help you to detect and prefer the nutritious compounds in meat. After all, in terms of how cats evolved, it is a waste of energy to hunt and kill animals that are not going to provide a high protein content. It is also of interest that you seem able to taste water, too.[19]

TOUCHING TOOLS – FUR AND PAWS

Finally, there is the fifth sense, the sense of touch. Your sense of touch, what you can feel on your skin, for instance, functions in much the same way as does the human sense of touch. The nerves in your skin transmit feelings of pain and pleasure to the brain and, like human skin, your skin responds to heat and cold. As your body temperature, at around 38.6°C (101.5°F), is higher than a human's, you can tolerate higher temperatures than a human can, although you suffer more in low temperatures, not least because your smaller size makes it more difficult to retain the heat in your body. This is one reason why you sleep on or even inside the bed with your human more often and more continuously in winter! You also have visible hair over almost all your body, which helps keep out the cold, compared to the tiny, almost invisible hairs on the human body. You do not need clothes – something that children sometimes forget when they try to dress up the family cat. When the weather changes, you can puff up your fur to keep warm. The tiny human hairs on the body also puff up in goosebumps, but this does not help to keep a human warm. When your feline fur stands upright, it is far more noticeable and more effective as insulation against the cold. It is a much easier way of thermoregulation than having to put on or remove clothes. Your fur, like human body hair, also stands up during emotional agitation.

Having hair almost all over your body, you feel the tiny touch sensations of the world around you that human clothes would block. On an ordinary non-pedigree cat, there are three different types of body hair – strong coarse guard hairs, medium awn hairs and soft short downy hairs on the bottom layer of your coat. (This varies in some pedigree cats bred to be hairless, or softer-haired.) At its root each hair has cells called *mechanoreceptors* that receive touch sensations when the hair moves. You can feel these when something brushes against your hair, bending it one way or another, as well as when something touches your actual skin. Humans experience something similar but only with the hair and skin that is not covered with clothes. The nerves at the roots of your body hairs can tell the difference between the light touch of the wind ruffling your fur, a light stroke by a human, or your fur getting tangled in a bramble.

The hair in the folds between your foot pad and toes is extra sensitive, with scores of nerve cells in every fold, which help when you use your front paws to pounce on a quivering mouse or poke a cat toy into movement – actions that a human would make with their hands. At the base of each claw is a further bunch of nerve ends which tell you if your claws are extended or retracted. According to Dr John Bradshaw, author of *The Behaviour of the Domestic Cat*, 'It is almost possible to think of the feet as sense organs in their own right, and their degree of sensitivity may explain why many cats appear to dislike having their paws touched.'[20]

BY A CAT'S WHISKER

One great advantage that you now have as a cat is that you have whiskers. These are stiff thick hairs that have a greater number of nerves at the base to send signals to the brain. They are finely tapered at the end and their proper, technical name is *vibrissae*, because, when they detect something, they vibrate. This vibration stimulates the sensitive nerves at the bottom of the whisker to transmit information to the brain. Your whiskers are so finely tuned and responsive that they can detect a change in air current, which tells them that they are near a solid object – rather like a radar detector. This helps you to hunt and to avoid bumping into things in the dark. You can also use your whiskers to work out if you can fit through a narrow passage – if you get through without your whiskers being touched, the rest of your body will follow without difficulty. Cats that are born blind compensate, at least in part, for their lack of sight by using their whiskers more.[21]

The main whiskers on your muzzle are mobile and can be swept backwards and forwards. If you are anxious or frightened, they will sweep backwards to stay out of range of damage, but they will swivel forwards if you are going on the offensive in a fight. If you have grabbed a mouse in your mouth, they sweep forwards so that they give you information about your struggling prey, information that your eyes cannot give you as they cannot see or focus that close. Whiskers on your forefeet, called *carpal hairs*, give similar information if you have grabbed the mouse with your paws, helping you tell whether it is wriggling so hard it might escape. Whiskers above your eyes protect them, triggering them to blink shut if something like long grass or other vegetation is close enough to injure you in the eye. The whiskers on your cheek may help you spread your scent when you rub your face against something.[22] Your whiskers are far superior to those in the static, relatively insensitive hairs in human facial hair! No human beard, however long or luxuriant, can compete with a cat's whiskers.

All in all, your five senses have been beautifully moulded by evolution to help you experience what is important for your survival in the world. They create and define your umwelt. They also have another function. They are valuable tools for communication, creating a language between you and other cats and between you and your human. This is the subject of our next chapter.

6

HOW YOU TALK AS A
CAT – WITH SOUND, BODY
LANGUAGE AND TOUCH

Humans talk with words; you communicate without words. You have a language, but you do not have words. You use sounds to communicate with other cats or with humans, just as human babies do, when they scream, grunt, chuckle or laugh, groan, sigh or squeal. Adult humans use these non-verbal sounds, too, but quite often add words to the sounds, words that have single elements of meaning that can be combined in thousands of different ways. As a cat, you *vocalize* – that is the correct scientific word – without any words.

Using vocal language is so important to humans that we will start with your feline vocal utterances, even though these may not be so vital to feline language. Silent language is a much safer way for a small animal like you to send a message than any vocal communication. Vocalizing loudly might catch the attention of a bigger predator like a dog or a coyote or a leopard, only to result in you becoming their next meal. Some of the big cats, jaguars, leopards, lions and tigers, free from fear of larger enemies, can roar loudly across long distances but do not purr. These big cats roar to scare off intruders or other cats. Other cats, mostly ones smaller than the big four (and that includes you!), purr but do not roar. Roaring would draw too much attention. However, you, as a domestic cat, probably use your voice more often than your solitary wild ancestor, *Felis sylvestris lybica*, did. And as a pet cat you often communicate vocally with your talkative humans, which suggests that domestication may have developed this tendency.[1]

To express your feelings or to communicate with others, you can purr, trill or chirrup, all noises made with your mouth closed. You can open your mouth to meow, chatter or chitter, and yowl or wail in various ways, then close it again to end the sound. Finally, you growl, snarl, hiss, spit and shriek with your mouth open, often showing your teeth, and teeth are usually a sign for others to be cautious in approaching you.[2] Putting your vocal language into these categories of whether your mouth is open or closed is one of the easiest for humans to understand, but scientists have suggested a variety of classifications, and, moreover, different individual cats use sounds differently, too. Now that digital recording is so easy, scientists can use audiographs to record your sounds. The recordings can be accurately studied in their visual diagrammatic form but are difficult to describe in ordinary human language.[3] Examples of the different cat sounds can be found on the excellent Meowsic website of Susanne Schötz, a feline vocalization researcher and best-selling author of *The Secret Language of Cats*.[4]

THE PURR

When you purr, most humans will enjoy the rhythmic sound. But how do you make this curious low sound? Humans cannot purr, however hard they try. Purring remains a bit of a mystery, although the scientific description of purring describes it this way: 'continuous sound production must alternate between pulmonic egressive and ingressive airstream (and usually go on for minutes)'.[5] Roughly what this means is that you can purr as you breathe out and also purr as you breathe in. This is unusual because many, though not all, animals only make sounds when they breathe out. Moreover, your continuous purring can go on for a long time. And purring volume and pitch are also, like everything else in your feline world, very individual. Some cats seem to purr louder on the in-breath, others on the out-breath. Some cats' purrs are very low; others' are a little higher in pitch. Some cats purr so quietly that it cannot be heard at all by humans. If you are a silent purrer, the vibrations can be either felt or just heard if a gentle human puts their ear close to your body. Some cats purr so loudly that the noise interferes with a veterinary surgeon's attempt to listen to their body sounds with a stethoscope.

And what are you saying when you purr? Kittens purr when they are suckling their mother, a close-range sound that is low enough and quiet enough not to alert predators. Possibly it is an 'all is well' reassuring sound or maybe a sound which says 'I am not a threat.'[6] Household cats often purr when they are contented or happy. However, some cats will purr when they are stressed or even when they are in pain or dying. Do you use that purr to soothe or calm yourself when you are ill? Or is it a care-eliciting purr, asking the vet to look after you? Or, because purring increases your breathing rate, is it a way of trying to make yourself feel less ill?[6] There is also another sort of purr with a cry inside it that you use to ask for something, usually food from your human.[7] It sounds quite urgent to a human, as indeed it is meant to! You also chirrup or trill to your kittens, and the kittens can tell your chirrup from the chirrups made by other cats.[8] You might even chirrup to your human, as some cats do.

THE MEOW

Of the sounds that you make when you open your mouth to articulate a message, then close it at the end, the meow is the most ambiguous and perhaps most flexible of feline sounds. Kittens meow to their mother, but adult cats rarely meow to each other. Nor is a meow used when a cat is in pain. The meow is normally saved for getting human attention. Because humans respond better to your vocal language than your body language, you learn that it can be used very effectively as a method of asking for food or petting. Indeed, you may develop different meows when, say, complaining to a human rather than requesting food. It is as if you develop an individual language for communicating to an individual human. Even if you were a feral cat that lived without or with very little human contact, you might learn to meow to the human feeders that turn up regularly. Some cats even do a silent meow, with the mouth opening and closing but making no sound. 'We have seen this in feral cats,' said Dr John Bradshaw, cat expert and the author of *Cat Sense*. 'Maybe the silent meow is just a visual signal.'[9]

How often and how noisily you meow is also influenced by your breed. Siamese cats and breeds developed from the Siamese are more likely to be very vocal to their owners. Susanne Schötz, who recorded 70 cats in their homes, concluded that there was a tendency for attention-seeking or happy meows to rise to higher notes, while stressed or unhappy meows fell to lower notes.[10] So your feelings are likely to influence your meows! Unsurprisingly, Dr Schötz found that kittens' meows were higher than adult cat meows. Another feature of the meow is how cats like you learn to use meows to communicate with their humans and how humans learn to interpret them. It seems that each cat has its own meow pattern, and which type of meow you use and in what circumstances depends on you having learned what meows have achieved in the past. Humans can often identify which meow is used in which context in their own cat but cannot do it for someone else's.[11] A remarkable example of this occurred in 2022 when a cat owner found her missing cat, Barnaby, by recognizing his individual meow in the background of a phone call. She had been calling the vet to check on her other cat, which was in for a procedure. She asked about a meow in the background. 'That's just a stray,' she was told. When she brought in photographs of the missing Barnaby, his identity was confirmed.[12]

OTHER CAT VOCALIZATIONS

You also make an open-mouth chatter a little like a stutter. This sounds a bit like a series of clicking noises, and you may do this without any of the vocal sound that occurs in a meow or yowl. You usually do this when you are looking through the window and outside is a bird or a mouse that you cannot get to. You express your frustration by using this odd sound. It is not a sound that you would make to a human or to another cat except in very unusual circumstances.

Then there are the louder noises that you make, when your feelings of sexual desire, frustration or terror become intense. Humans categorize these in several different terms. There is the sexual call of male cats that have not been castrated, sometimes called a *caterwaul* or a *mowl*, and the sexual call of female cats, sometimes called a *yowl*. These can be throaty or higher pitched, short or long, in a series of mowls or yowls to attract a mate. You also make a noisy yowl or howl when you are facing up to enemy cats that you might be about to fight with or have fought with in the past. These angry howls also vary in pitch and in duration. It is as if the importance and excitement of mate searching or the desire to see off a rival overcome the normal caution which usually keeps feline vocal language relatively quiet.

The aggression yowls can go on for a long time and may be interspersed with short bouts of close combat. The same lack of feline caution applies to the open-mouth shriek you may give when hurt or when actually engaged in cat combat. When you growl your mouth may sometimes be closed, sometimes open, and a growl is a warning to an opponent, whether feline or human. You also spit, snarl and hiss. The open-mouth hiss gives a visible warning message as well by showing the teeth.

BODY LANGUAGE

Even if you are living in a peaceful human suburb, any loud sounds you make put you at risk of attack from a predator, whether this is a dog, a fox or a human throwing a brick at you. That is why much of the time you use body language rather than sounds to express yourself to both humans and other cats. Body language is silent and therefore safer. It can be friendly, neutral or threatening. Some of your body language is known to and studied by humans, but your feline body language is often too subtle to be easy for a human either to understand or to study. Humans who want to know what you are saying need to look at all your body movements, even the smaller ones, not just focus on one obvious signal.

Your body language will mean different things according to context. If you are running up a tree, you might be escaping from a dog at the base of the tree; you might be in pursuit of a bird in the higher branches; or you might just be playing zoomies – that is, rushing around for fun. Temperature will also make a difference. When it is cold, you curl into a tight ball, wrapping your tail around your body; when it is hot, you lie stretched out. For example, in a house with central heating you will often lie on your back under a radiator with your belly positioned upwards to get the heat. However, if the temperature is a steady neutral one, being spread out or tightly curled up may be a way of expressing your emotions.

Let us look more carefully at one particular bit of body language to see how circumstances may alter the message. What are you saying when you turn on your side and expose your belly? Exposing your tender belly, where there usually isn't much protective fur, makes you vulnerable. It would be nice for human observers if the spread-out belly flop had only one meaning, but it has more. It can be the 'social roll' when you are being friendly towards a human. You are not necessarily inviting the human to rub your belly, however – as they will find out if they try! You might also roll on your side or back during a play session with another cat, inviting it to pounce on you for another bout of playing. When you are playing on your own with a cat toy or a dead mouse, you might roll on your back, exposing your belly, and juggle the toy with your paws. You might also lie on your side in a half- or full-roll position with your claws ready to defend yourself if another aggressive cat is standing over you.

This roll would not make you vulnerable if your claws were already protracted ready to scratch. It would be a defensive posture, which allows you to have all the claws in your four paws weaponized ready to repel an attack. A roll like this in a similar situation might also be a sign of submission or subordination, though some cat experts have argued that, as a cat, you do not signal subordination to other cats under any circumstances.

So, there are at least five ways you express yourself, when you roll on your side in front of either a cat or a human – five meanings to one particular bit of body language. This is not unlike human verbal language where a word, a phrase or a sentence can have several different meanings. If one human says to another, 'You are awful,' it might be a loving remark or a playful one or an aggressive insult depending on the context, tone of voice and what the two people are doing at the time. So, in a similar way, if you make a particular body language movement it has to be understood by humans, and no doubt other cats, in the light of the whole situation. The 'social roll' can be friendly, playful towards another cat, part of playing with an object, defensive, or even perhaps a way of showing that you do not want to fight. Just as humans have a limited number of words, so you have a limited number of behaviours you can use for communication, so context and other less obvious additional features, like the state of your claws, add further meaning.

FACIAL EXPRESSIONS

Humans detect what other humans are feeling by looking at their face. And many can read the face of the family dog quite well, too. Dogs can grin in a kind of smile, raise their eyebrows, and pucker their noses in movements that help humans read what is going on in the canine mind. Your feline face seems relatively inexpressive to many humans, though there is now a standardized coding system called *CatFACS* (www.catfacs.com) which allows specially trained scientists to track the small facial muscle changes that reflect your feelings. As mentioned earlier, cats operate in a faster world, and so can see, in the blink of an eye, things that a human might miss. Presumably, other cats can read your more subtle facial movements just as ordinary humans can read the subtle movements of the human face. Scientists have been studying your facial expressions since the 1950s and come up with some of your (to humans) more recognizable facial expressions.[13]

The facial language that is most obvious to humans, and that can be seen at quite a distance by another cat, is the movement of your ears. Humans with their fixed ears cannot express themselves this way! When you are frightened, your ears flatten along the side of your face, and if you are likely to attack, your ears will swivel backwards. Sometimes, as the emotions come and go, one ear will change posture while the other stays the same.[14]

Your eyes also tell what is going on inside your mind. Your whole eye widens and gets rounder if you are aroused, surprised or triggered into a strong emotional reaction; it narrows back to its normal almond shape when you are feeling ordinary contentment. Your pupils also enlarge with emotional arousal or contract into a normal shape with relaxation. If you are concentrating and thinking of either pouncing on a mouse or attacking a feline enemy, your eyes contract slightly in a kind of hard continuous stare. You may get into a staring match with another cat, both of you locked into hostile eye contact. Blinking and head turning is one way of breaking off mutual staring between you and another cat, when the staring is getting too threatening for you.

Rapid half blinks are a sign of fear, so might be a subtle movement of your eyes and head to the left, according to recent researchers.[15] Why turn the head and eyes to the left? The right side of the brain is what you use to process a response to negative unpleasant stimuli and controls the left side of your body. Long slow blinking towards a human, on the other hand, is a sign of affectionate relaxation.[16] Your eyes half blink and narrow slowly, sometimes closing completely, and then repeat the action. Even the least observant humans will sometimes notice and enjoy this.

TALL TAILS

You also use your tail to send a message, both to humans and to other cats. The advantage of a tail signal is that it can be read from a distance. If you hold your tail up high – the 'tail-up' signal – it means friendship. Cats will walk towards their humans or towards other cats, and even from a distance that silent tail signal can be easily read. You may have a small kink backwards, forwards or even sideways in that tail, and some cats move their tail forwards along their back with a larger curve so that the tail almost looks like the curly tail of a Spitz-type dog. Of course, if you are a Manx cat, you do not have a tail, so tail signals will not be in your repertoire. Another friendly tail gesture is the tail wrap. As you walk beside another cat with both your tails up, you intertwine your tail with theirs in a tail wrap, sometimes rubbing your two flanks against each other at the same time.

In ordinary circumstances, your tail hangs loose and it will move upwards, sideways or downwards to help you balance as you walk, run or jump. When you feel fear, however, you may tuck your tail between your legs to protect your backside, and perhaps to tell an enemy that you are not going to attack. Or, if you are crouching or sitting, you wrap it tightly around your body as protection. Your tail will also tell when you are thinking of attacking another cat. It rises upwards from the base and then turns down again in a downward loop not unlike the top of a traditional human walking stick. All the fur on it stands up, so it looks like a bristle brush. That is part of making yourself look threatening to an opponent. You also swish your tail as a warning signal during a hostile encounter or to show you are thinking of biting your human. If the human petting you notices that tail swishing, it is a sign to take away their hand before they get nipped; it is an indication that you are frustrated or angry. When you twitch your tail only slightly, it is not a sign of a particular negative emotion, just that you are interested, intrigued or concentrating on something.

BODY POSTURE

Your overall body posture also tells other cats and humans what is going on. If you are frightened, you lower your body towards the ground, pull back your whiskers, put your tail between your legs, flatten your ears against your head, and shrink away from what is frightening you. You make yourself look small and unthreatening to any potential opponent. Running away may invite pursuit and, if you are caught, an attack. Often, if you are really terrified, you will just freeze without moving. The message is: 'I don't want to provoke you.'

If you want to deter an attack or threaten another cat or even a dog, you make yourself look large. You may also turn sideways to your opponent to show how big your body is. The message is: 'I am big and powerful, so don't mess with me.' This big-body posture, combined with a hard stare, ears swivelled back, a lashing tail and a loud howling noise, is designed to intimidate. This may be enough to deter a rival so that he moves away. He will usually slink away very slowly so as not to trigger your chase impulse. As well as the big-body appearance, you often raise a paw – a gesture that is designed to tell an opponent that you are ready to scratch. The raised paw may be made either by an attacker or by a defender. In dogs, a paw raise has been classified as an appeasement gesture; in cats, it is the exact opposite. It is a threat, although just to confuse human onlookers, it can also be used to entice play as well.

If you are unlucky enough to have found yourself homeless and are waiting for adoption in an animal rescue centre, your body postures will show whether you are distressed or relaxed.[17] A way of deciding how stressed and fearful you are has been worked out by scientists who have looked at all the details of your body language. A relaxed cat lies on its side exposing its belly, breathing slowly, with its legs and tail extended, head lying down, eyes closed or half closed, pupils normal, ears and whiskers normal, silent and at rest. At the other extreme, the terrified cat is crouched in a hunched, tense position with its four legs below it (ready to flee), tail close to the body, head lowered, eyes and pupils wide, ears flattened, and whiskers swept back against the face. If it can, this terrified cat will be either hiding in its closed sleeping area, or lowering itself inside its cat box, or even hiding underneath a bit of bedding. These are the extremes of a cat's reaction to being put into an unfamiliar pen. As a tool for deciding whether a cat is emotionally suffering, this stress score should be taught to rescue-shelter staff, but it is a skill that takes many hours to perfect.

KEEPING YOUR DISTANCE . . . OR NOT

Perhaps your most obvious use of body language is the use of distance. Thanks to your evolutionary past as a loner, you are an expert at social distancing. When you come across an unknown cat or sometimes an unknown human, you stop and look from afar. You gaze for a very long time, if necessary, before walking forwards or retreating. Distance means safety. Distance also is the way you deal with conflict. You do not usually want to start a fight, so you will space yourself so that you do not come into close contact with cats that you do not like. Within a house you will spend time in a separate room, or on separate armchairs, or different windowsills. In extreme circumstances you might cower right at the far end underneath the bed or retreat to the top of the highest wardrobe to keep away from a resident feline enemy. If you share a human bed with another resident cat, you may keep a distance in order not to be too close, and you may carefully turn your back to them. The distance you keep from another cat is often proportionate to the friendliness or unfriendliness of your relationship with them.

Of course, you may have a feline friend, usually a sibling or a cat with whom you spent time in kittenhood. Apart from the tail-up and tail wrap, what are the other signs that cats like each other? The language of friendship is often tactile, because, if you like another cat, you can risk getting close and personal rather than having to keep a safe distance. When you meet up, you will often touch noses in greeting rather as human beings give warm, close handshakes rather than more distant formal ones. Just like human friends, you and your feline friends (if you have any – some cats are loners that don't) often hang out together. If you like another cat, you will frequently sleep or rest together with an area of your bodies touching. You are sharing the emotional warmth of friendship, not just body warmth. With a human that you like, you may sleep or rest on their lap or merely sit so close on the sofa that your body is touching theirs. At night you have a choice of how close you want to sleep, and it is influenced not just by how cold the bedroom is but also how close your mutual relationships are. Many cats will sleep on the bed with their human inside it. You might sleep right on top of the human body or snuggle down inside the bedclothes, stretching out to align your body against the human body, or you might even sleep in human arms.

You rub against your feline friend, using your head, cheeks or flanks usually after approaching each other with the raised tail-up signal. You rub against humans, too. It is common for cats like you to rub their bodies against human legs when you want to be fed. You might even rub your face against the human face or push your head against your human in what is known as *bunting*. These tactile messages are the equivalent of human handholding, hugs or social kisses. When you are very relaxed and happy you use your front paws to knead, rhythmically treading whatever surface you are on while extending and retracting your claws and purring. This is what you did as a kitten when you were suckling from your mother, as the movements may have stimulated her to let down milk. Sometimes, as an adult you will knead on an inanimate soft surface, but sometimes you will knead on a human body, usually the lap. Occasionally, even as an adult you will knead on another cat or even on a canine buddy. This is an expression of pleasure and relaxation which sends a message that says you are behaving like a kitten, a signal that strengthens the bond between cat and human.

The other message of friendship is when you groom another cat, usually a relation or sometimes just a familiar friend.[18] The technical name for this is *allogrooming,* and it is what a mother cat does to clean up her kittens. If you and another adult are friends, you may do it to your feline buddy or social partner who may sometimes reciprocate. Allogrooming is usually enjoyed by the cat being groomed, but it can end in a kind of spat, if you groom too long or if you pin down the other cat to stop it leaving.[19] Allogrooming, according to ethologists, is a way of strengthening social bonds between cats. Occasionally, you groom humans, too, which can be very uncomfortable for them, particularly if you groom a male on his bald head. Finally, another sign of affection is rough-and-tumble play. The body language you show during this kind of play can confuse human onlookers. Your ears may go back, you may lift a paw, you may body-slam the other player, do a defensive roll on your back, and even seem to be biting your opponent. It looks like fighting, except that each player comes back for more after a short pause, both cats take turns to make various moves, and there is no blood on the carpet. Most important of all, this play fighting is silent – unless it gets too rough and one of the players makes a vocal protest, to put an end to the play.[20]

Finally, there are the tactile messages of nipping, biting and scratching. You may use your mouth to hold on to a body part, without any biting pressure. This is the mildest form of deterrence, sometimes used during allogrooming when a cat tries to move away from the groomer. It is also used as a signal to petting humans, to say that they should stop their stroking. Nips that do not break the skin are another way you tell a human to stop what it is doing. You may also use this on a friendly cat that is grooming you or during mutual play. These are not proper bites, although they may precede a more serious bite. You may give a deep bite if you are terrified and/or enraged, cornered or unable to escape. In a real fight you can severely damage or be damaged by another cat, and uncastrated street tomcats often display the wounds and scars from their fights. Scratching also causes real damage. At close quarters a raking scratch from your hindlegs can catch the other cat's soft belly.

Full-on fighting between cats does occur, but is not as common as might be expected. Many cats seem aggressive to each other when they are simply saying, 'I no longer want to play with you.' This does not mean their relationship has broken down. In a true threat, there is often a long stand-off with posturing and howling and pausing, which can allow for either cat to withdraw. Normally, they do so slowly to avoid an attack, but if the environment allows escape, they might go for the quick dash. Avoidance is the way cats prefer to deal with conflict, and they have ways to ensure fights are kept to a minimum in ordinary daily circumstances. Visual body language, unlike tactile contact or even vocal communication, allows cats to communicate while practising social distancing. Even so, body language still requires cats to be within sight of each other.

However, there is a way you can leave messages for other cats when they are not even in sight. This is what we will turn to in the next chapter.

7

HOW AS A CAT YOU TALK WITH SCENT – YOUR SECRET LANGUAGE

L ike humans, you can leave messages which other cats can read
remotely. You may have to share some of your range with other
cats. You don't want to meet close-up with most of them, or
perhaps with any of them. You want to be able to hunt alone without
a rival taking the prey off you. You also do not want to be detected
by a scary dog or coyote or dingo which might hurt and injure you.
True, you do not do letters, email, phone calls, WhatsApp, TikTok,
EliteSingles or Facebook posts. But what you do have is the ability to
post on what might be called Nosebook or FelineSingles, or send a
'peemail' – that is, a urine scent mark.

Scent marks are ideal for a small animal like you which needs to
communicate with your fellow cats. Scent marks are silent. They are
therefore safe. They can be left for other cats to read when you are no
longer there, so they minimize the risk of conflict, while providing
you with reassurance. They can give a variety of messages. They can
also be used like sticky notes or diary reminders for yourself rather
than messages to other cats. They can be used like a route marker,
marking paths that you use, reminding you where you are, where

you have been and when you were there, rather like an edit history on a Facebook post. Scent messages can be used like the dating site EliteSingles as a method of looking for a suitable mate. They also have signatures, saying who left them. They are long lasting. They are even time stamped, like the top of a human email. A scent mark is what lots of animal species use for messaging, not just cats. Mice, rats, rabbits and even big cats like lions and tigers use them. Whenever you are exploring new territory or patrolling your existing territory, you will be sniffing the air and objects to see if there are any new scent messages, in the same way that humans check their email, text messages or WhatsApp.

MAKING SCENT MARKS – A GUIDE FOR BEGINNERS

So how do you do make a scent mark? You use body odour and body fluids to leave a message. Scent marks can be made up of two kinds of odour: your ordinary individual body odours or pheromones, which are special scents common to all cats. The ordinary body odours are those you share with all animals, including humans – mouth odour, breath odour, skin odour, sweat odour, genital odour, anal odour, and odour from ears and hair. Some of these odours will be more noticeable when you have bad teeth, indigestion, ear infections or skin infections. These odours are not specifically developed for leaving messages but can still be picked up by others. You produce these odours wherever you go and wherever you are – from your mouth, ears, paw pads and the rest of your body. The odours of your bodily fluids – urine, faeces and saliva – are also individual to you and so can be used to detect your presence or recent presence in an area, whether you like it or not. Thus, there are traces of your scent wherever you

Above: An artist's reconstruction of *Proailurus lemanensis*, the first cat-type ancestor of all modern feline species, including domestic cats. The size of a modern bobcat, *Proailurus* lived in Europe more than 25 million years ago.

Left: This cat is keeping itself warm by sleeping in a curled-up position. It has wrapped its tail, head and three paws round its belly, in order to insulate an area where there is less fur.

Right: Cats feel safer high up. This sleeping cat has a spread-out body, showing its belly, with one front paw stretched out and the other under the chest. This elongated position shows that the cat is both warm and relaxed in its environment.

One day old

Ten days old

Three weeks old

Five weeks old

Fourteen weeks old

Five months old

Adult cat

Kittens develop from the first day of life without sight or hearing and with limited movement, to independent hunting around five months. Females can be sexually fertile after three months and males after six months. Complete social maturity takes several more months.

A cat's view (top) versus a human's view (below). Because humans and cats see things from different heights, the cat cannot see the tomatoes on the table, so we shouldn't be surprised when it jumps up to investigate these surfaces. We both have a central area of relatively high definition (although not as great in the cat) with most of our visual field actually being quite poorly defined. The positioning of the eyes means that cats have a slightly wider field of view and the reflective surface at the back of their eyes means things appear much brighter in daylight, with what's outside the window bleached out. However, cats can see more definition in the darker areas of the image. Cats also have a degree of colour blindness, so reds are less vibrant.

Above: A cat in hunting mode with ears forwards, eyes wide, focused on its prey and with its body tense waiting to pounce. Hunting is essential for survival for feral cats and arouses the pleasurable emotion of desire in all cats, even if they are regularly fed by humans.

Above: This is the tail-up greeting signal from a cat walking towards its human. Tail-up is a message of friendship that can be read at a distance. The tail says that coming close is safe and desirable. The tip can kink sideways, forwards or backwards.

Left: This cat is making itself look as big as possible by arching its back and standing on tiptoe. The fur on its back and tail stands up to increase the size of its body. With ears slightly lowered, the message is: 'Don't mess with me.'

Right: When a cat rolls on to its back, the roll can have several different meanings. Rolling is often a friendly gesture, but this cat has its claws out on one front paw, ready to defend itself in an uncertain social encounter, if its friendly message and request for distance are not respected.

Above: Social play fighting between cats can be difficult to distinguish from real fighting. Social play fights look rough but are generally silent or at least lack vocal threats. Playing cats keep claws retracted and take turns to attack. In a real fight, claws are out and there is often a lot of noise.

Right: Playing with a moving ball or a toy, known as object play, is the next best thing to hunting for a cat. It arouses the same emotion of pleasurable desire. To make a ball move, the cat will poke it with its paw. Cats are fascinated by the physics of force and motion, as this makes them better hunters, so they will often push things off a shelf so see how much effort is required to get different objects to move in certain ways.

Cats express themselves with body language. Signals from tail, ears and body movements send messages to other cats and to humans at a distance.

FRIENDLY

The tail straight up with a kink at the top is a greeting signal, showing that a cat is friendly towards its human.

DEFENSIVE

A bottle-brush tail, fur raised on back, and a slightly arched back indicate high arousal and a willingness to fight if needs be.

CURIOUS

The tail hangs loose, ears are forward, body straight as a cat shows interest, investigates and patrols to check for any changes in its territory.

ANXIOUS

The upright quivering tail without spraying is when a cat is excited but cannot get what it wants (e.g. before feeding). A sign of anticipation that can spill into frustration and may result in a spray of urine.

RELAXED

The tail lying flat and the body spread out with paws tucked under show that a cat is feeling safe and tranquil. If it changes position as you approach, then it is not so comfortable in your presence.

UNEASY

The lowered tail with slight upward curve at the base with ears moving backwards signals that a cat is feeling fearful. Slow movement aims to reduce tension and the risk of an attack from another cat.

FEARFUL

The lowered ears, the tail tucked between legs to protect the backside, and body slightly arched are signs that a cat is feeling fear.

ANGRY

The ears are swivelled back and the tail is lashing side to side, showing that a cat is feeling frustrated and angry, so might attack.

EXCITED

The tail twitches with excitement, ears are forward with attentiveness, as a cat pokes something small to make it move during object play.

JOYFUL

A cat gambolling or bounding with pleasure has ears forward and tail held high above the ground, then curving downwards.

Above: Grooming another cat, known as allogrooming, indicates that cats like each other and is thought to strengthen their bond. Sometimes the groomer will use a paw to hold down the cat being groomed. Allogrooming may end in what might look like a brief quarrel, if the groomed cat has had enough, but that is just a cat's way of saying, 'No more, and I'm not moving!'

Left: When a cat rubs against human legs, it is often asking for attention. It is also depositing its own scent there and picking up the human's scent. This odour mixture makes up a family scent, the reassuring scent of safe territory.

Left: Scratching conditions the front claws, stretches the muscles (especially after sleeping) and also leaves a visual cue to scent messages from the feet for other cats. Conflict between resident cats or punishment by humans will increase a cat's need to scratch.

Below: Staring hard, as the ginger-and-white cat is doing, is intimidating. The black cat is defensive, with ears swivelled back, lowered tail, raised fur and a slightly arched back to display its strength. The black slowly retreats as he has decided he doesn't want to fight.

go, but you can also use these fluids to leave a deliberate scent mark. A blend of all these odours creates what is called a *signature mixture*, which specifically identifies you and your status (e.g. gender, age, fitness and reproductive status) as an individual to other cats.[1] Even humans can recognize your signature scent in heavily scented places such as a not very clean cat bed, and if you live with another cat, most human owners can, if they bother, distinguish between the two of you by scent. A signature mixture applies to other individuals, too. Within the household each human and the family dog will have a signature scent that you will recognize as familiar. The overall group smell of all animals, humans and familiar household smells is also a signature mixture for the home and family.

The scents that you leave can also include *pheromone mixtures*. These will not identify you as an individual, but they boost emotional responses such as sexual desire, a feeling of security, a feeling that 'Mummy is here – all is well', feelings of alarm, and other responses that are not yet fully understood in detail.[2] As we have said earlier, these are specific to your species, normally produced and detected only by you and other cats. They are social odours that convey information that can only be read by another cat, odours that humans cannot detect. These pheromone smells are not individualized, but general. However, the nature or strength of them will add to your odour assessment by another cat.

For example, if you are on a vet's examination table, you might read the message from the scent left by a previous cat. Your assessment might be: 'This is a scent left by a cat I don't recognize, and he was alarmed when he left it!' This strange cat smell would tell you that the preceding cat was not familiar, and the sweat off the paw pads and perhaps an alarm pheromone would predispose you to feel fear.[3] There would also be other, ordinary veterinary smells in the surgery, which you have learned by experience to associate with being stabbed by a vaccination needle – smells of disinfectant, medicines, dogs, strange humans. Everything about the smellscape in the surgery may feel threatening to you. No wonder that you, like most cats, are frightened in the vet's surgery.

Your own scent marks often include both your signature scent and a pheromone. Many of them come from skin glands.[4] Facial pheromone-emitting glands are found on the skin round your face, under your chin, at the corners of your mouth, on either side of your forehead, and on your cheeks. There are also potential pheromone glands on the base of your paw pads, where you sweat, and between the toes. There are pheromone glands on the upper surface of the base of your tail. (These glands are visible in uncastrated toms that develop 'stud tail'.) There are also glands in the skin below the tail near your anus. Along the gentle groove between your two rows of nipples are glands that excrete a pheromone starting about three days after a litter of kittens has been born and ending a few days after their weaning. Around the genital area you have more pheromone-producing glands which are not well studied.[5]

SENDING MESSAGES

To sum up, your scent messages say who you are with a signature-mixture odour and can convey a message with a pheromone that is important for you as a cat. So, how do you leave a scent message? There are several methods you can use.

Facial marking is a way of scent marking that even the least observant human usually notices, and it is sometimes called *bunting*. When you rub your face to leave a scent mark, you are depositing not just the ordinary signature scent of your face but also the pheromones from the glands on your face and mouth. Scientists have identified five different chemical mixtures making up your facial pheromones which are found in a facial mark. The function of three of them is well known. One of these chemical mixtures is used by an uncastrated tomcat, probably to advertise their sexual status and desirability. Another is a component used to mark places and items in a way that flags them up as familiar. A third component is rubbed on familiar cats, dogs or people to mark them as friends. Your feline friends are often cats that you have known since kittenhood or that for some reason you find compatible.

Remember, as your vision is not very good, using scent is a much more efficient way of creating a familiar environment and defining safe areas in an ever-changing world. Face rubbing on another cat or a human is important for feline harmony and contentment. So are other ways you deposit scent.

There are some other ways of spreading the ordinary signature scent from your body in addition to face rubbing. You often sleep touching your feline friends or humans, sharing the warmth and the smell of the bed. That contact also deposits your scent, as does the flank rubbing and tail wrapping that you do with your feline friends. Indeed, the tail wrapping may also spread some of the pheromone that is emitted by the glands at the base of your tail. You may also groom a cat friend and therefore spread the scent of your saliva on his or her body.[6] When you meet up with another friendly cat, you usually sniff. You sniff nose to nose, or you sniff the backside.

You may be checking that they smell correctly for a cat in your personal group of friends or if they have been in contact with another cat outside the group.

You can detect all this because, when you make close contact with another cat or a human, you pick up the scent of those individuals at the same time as depositing your own scent. That means your body will have some of your cat friends' scent and the scent of any human or dog you have rubbed. So, all your facial scent marks become a mixture of your scent and their scents, making up a reassuring identifying scent for your group. This family or group scent, with its feelings of security and group belonging, can be disrupted by the arrival of strange cats, or cats that come home smelling of the vet, or humans that bring back worrying smells from their work or other activity – hospital odours, for example, smell rather like vets' surgeries. You will also notice changes in the family scent if one of your co-resident cats dies, if a new partner moves in, if your human gets pregnant, or when a new baby arrives.

Any disruption of or change in the household group scent like this may prompt you to go round depositing or topping up your facial scent marks on your environment as a way of improving the family scent profile. It might be that you also do this by adding a urine mark which may either strengthen the signal or provide reassurance. However, the places where you deposit your facial scent marks are those that are familiar and safe and therefore you do not need to mark them more prominently with urine or scratching. As a domestic cat you will rub your face in your core territory, usually the house or apartment where you live with your owner. You will rub on the corner of door frames, on skirting boards, on the side of windowsills, stairs, on armchairs, sofas, chairs, human beds, cupboards, table legs, the lower half of fridge doors, and even on desktop computers. You top up these scent marks by more rubbing when they begin to fade. All this creates that group scent profile important in your safe living area. When an interfering human cleans them off, you have to re-mark them to restore the odour of home comfort and security.[7]

You may also feel the need to rub against new items in the home or even shopping bags that are brought in from outside, to make sure they smell of home. These may smell of the outside unfamiliar world, and if you are a sensitive cat, you will feel they need marking to make them become part of home. A worrying scenario for you is when a Christmas tree that has been sold off the street is taken into the household. A passing dog may have urinated on it while it was outside on the pavement before being sold. Another stressful scenario is when a shopping bag is placed on the house step, while the human opens the door with a key. By chance the bag may have been put down on a step where a passing dog has lifted his leg or a local cat has urinated. It will then smell to you of dog or a strange cat. In this case you may feel you need to make a stronger marking effort on the shopping bag. A face rub may not be enough.

THE FINE ART OF URINATING

This is where urine comes into your scent-marking repertoire. Humans really notice the smell of cat urine, although they normally have no idea what the scent marks mean to you. However, for you, urine carries a lot of information about other cats. It contains a pungent chemical called *felinine* and can be used to smother other scents. The amount of felinine varies according to your gender, age and – somewhat bizarrely – your type of coat. (This is due to sulphur being present in both felinine and the proteins making up hair.) The urine of entire male cats contains the most felinine, which may explain the pungent 'tomcat odour' so disliked by humans. There is less felinine in the urine of castrated males, even less in unspayed females, while spayed females have the least and kittens none at all.[8] Felinine also degrades over time. So, a good sniff of another cat's urine deposit will tell you whether the individual is familiar or unfamiliar and how long ago the urine was deposited.[9] For an animal that wants to avoid conflict living in an area which is used by several cats, this information is important to you. It allows you to avoid known rivals and be cautious about stranger cats that might be aggressive. It is a message that is relatively long lasting and one that allows communication at both a physically and a temporally safe distance.

In normal circumstances you urinate by squatting on the ground. If there is something like soil to dig into, you dig a hole using your front paws, then balance your backside over the hole to urinate into it. If you are not in a hurry, you will often turn to inspect it and start covering up the urine with the soil. If you need to urinate on a hard surface, you will not be able to dig but you will often do a few scratches as if you were able, because this is the hard-wired ritual. Since most cats stay within their core territory and hunting range, it makes sense to cover up the waste products for hygienic reasons. You will normally urinate away from the core area where you shelter or are fed,[10] in a location where you will not be disturbed. Just like most humans, you prefer to toilet in privacy and without interruption.

However, when you specifically use urine to scent mark areas, rather than just relieve yourself, this almost always involves a different sort of location, one which will get attention. You choose a specific object like a tree or a wall, often backing up against it and spraying urine horizontally out of your backside, although sometimes instead you crouch over horizontal surfaces to mark them with urine. If you are standing up to scent mark, your tail is lifted vertically and, as you spray, the top of your tail quivers. Sometimes you narrow your eyes, as if you are concentrating. You do not cover up this urine deposit. Indeed, where you choose to urine mark often involves a conspicuous location or an object like a prominent plant or low branch which will be noticed by other cats. You will repeatedly urine mark this location to update the information of when you were there and to prolong the persistence of the scent mark. Interestingly, unlike male dogs that almost queue up to lift their legs on the same object, you do not routinely feel the need to spray mark over a mark left by another male cat, although you may use urine to smother other unfamiliar scents.[11] You repeat-spray over your own spray marks, topping them up as if updating them. This kind of spray marking will contain pheromones and is done most often by uncastrated male cats and also, though less often, by unneutered females that are on heat. About 5–10 per cent of neutered cats, both male and female, will also frequently spray in certain circumstances. While sexual marks tend to be short and sweet, territorial marks may involve very large amounts of urine.

For unneutered cats on the feline dating scene at the right time of year, sprayed urine can act like the photograph on a human internet dating site. You leave a pheromone scent mark saying you are looking for a mate, and you can read a pheromone scent mark left by another cat to assess whether that cat is a potential partner.

Your spray marking is also connected to the fact that you have a known hunting range and are not normally very sociable towards other cats. You have a core territory (usually in the house if you are a domestic cat) and a hunting range outside the house which overlaps with the range of other cats. Your spray marks are not a simple Keep Out noticeboard to other cats. You do not erect a fence of urine spray marks at the edge of a fixed territory. Instead, you spray mark in the paths you use within that range, probably to help you time-share locations with other cats. Your spray marks are time-stamped, telling others when you were present at the location, perhaps allowing other cats to avoid a conflict. Other cats will sniff and inspect your marks, but are not necessarily deterred by them.[12] Your marks may also act as a sticky note for yourself, reminding you when you were last there, and possibly flagging up a site that requires a certain caution or one that you need to remember for some other reason.

If you are a neutered cat living in a household, you will not be spraying urine to find a mate, but may be doing so due to social anxiety or concern about 'your' property and possessions. You are more likely to spray urine to mark territory if you live with other cats in the same house than if you are a solitary pet, suggesting that in a multi-cat household there may be competition for access to litter trays or other resources, or occasional falling out among the feline residents.[13] You may also choose to spray near doors or windows, if you are having social difficulties with cats outside the house, particularly if you have free access via a cat flap to a neighbourhood with many other pet cats.[14] If you do resort to spray marking, it seems possible that depositing your own urine scent is comforting and helps you cope in some way. You will normally top up and update these marks regularly, so you must get some advantage from doing this; otherwise you would not bother. Humans still do not fully understand exactly why you are spraying. However, if the source of your stress is taken away, and the spray marks removed, you should not need to spray mark.

FAECES – BURIED OR UNBURIED?

The other way to deposit a strong scent mark is to leave your faeces lying around where they can be sniffed. Usually, you are careful to defecate away from any food area in a relatively undisturbed place, and if there is a suitable surface you will dig a hole, defecate and cover it up (you prefer to urinate and defecate in different locations given the choice). Sometimes you leave your faeces uncovered simply because you are defecating on a hard surface or because you do not want to use the litter tray. But at other times you are deliberately scent marking with faeces. The odours from this can convey useful information to other cats. In a similar way, you will sometimes sniff the bottom of another cat, usually a familiar one, because the odours at the backside give you information you do not get from a mere visual encounter. (You do this far less frequently than dogs, however, because you are more cautious about getting close to strange cats.) So, it is not surprising that any exposed faeces will be of interest to you and other cats as a socially distanced form of information.

Like other carnivores you have a pair of anal sacs that release a pungent odour into your faeces. This odour of your anal sac secretions has been analysed by researchers, who have concluded that it identifies the individual cat.[15] While the solids in faeces can vary according to what you have eaten, your anal sac odour stays the same and marks the faeces as your very own. This anal sac odour is one of the scents that other cats are interested in when they sniff your backside. It is possible they are double-checking something about your identity rather than checking up on your sexual status.[16]

Your solid faeces not only include the anal sac information, but also contain chemicals that inform other cats that this is another cat and that it is either male or female.[17] One of these chemicals is a derivative from felinine, which is also found in urine. This derivative, MMB (in full: 3-mercapto-3-methylbutan-1-ol), is a pheromone that tells you whether the depositor is male or, in its absence, female. Male cats have been shown to detect this chemical better than females. This MMB odour may be important for males that wish to avoid confrontation with rivals in overlapping territory.[18] Like spray marks, faeces are long lasting and are also time-stamped and can tell you when they were deposited.

But if you leave your faeces unburied or in a prominent site, how far does this deter cats from entering an area? Researchers have come up with different findings on the issue of buried versus unburied faeces and exactly how or if the placement of unburied faeces is a territorial mark.[19] If you leave your faeces unburied, it conveys a social and time message for any other cats, but if you are a free-roaming feral cat, the effect of this message still remains to be clarified. And, of course, sometimes the place you deposit faeces may just be unsuitable for digging anyway. However, if you are a household cat living in a multi-cat household and thus in close contact with other cats, unburied faeces outside the litter tray may occur for a different reason. The anal gland odour of another cat's faeces in the litter tray may deter you from adding your own into the same tray.[20] When researchers sprayed a synthetic anal gland odour on litter trays, cats were deterred from using it for their own faeces, although they still used the tray for urination. This runs counter to an earlier study,[21] so it is clear that humans still do not fully understand your faeces communication system.

SCRATCHING – THE CAT'S RUNES

Some of your cat messages use more than one medium, like the meow which may be a visual message of an open and closing mouth, as well as a sound communication. Scratching is another form of language that combines both a visual and a scent message. Outdoor cats scratch on tree trunks, while cats that live in the house scratch on sofas, chairs, carpets, curtains, wooden objects, sisal rope and door and window frames. Cats tend to have a preference both for the surface they scratch and the site where they scratch. They return to the same place to scratch on top of the existing scratch marks. The claw marks may be a visual attraction to the chemical message.

You scratch not only to sharpen your claws and to get rid of any old claw sheaths but also in order to exercise your body and forelimbs or to leave a chemical message. Sometimes you just scratch on a horizontal surface like a carpet or a cardboard box, but another way to get a good scratch is to use a vertical surface, where you can get a really good stretch for your spine. Female cats scratch on household items as much as male cats, and neutering does not make you scratch either more or less.[22] Even cats that have suffered declawing (in those countries where this operation is still legal) go through the motions of scratching, because the actions are hard-wired into their repertoire,[23] and they presumably can still leave a chemical message, if not its visual counterpart.

Thus, scratching also has an important signalling function. When you scratch you leave behind an odour from the scent glands on your paw pads and on the skin between the toes. You also leave visible scratch marks where you scratch, and you often do this on a prominent position that can be seen by other cats. Both the scent and the visual marks persist for a long time, as cat owners with scratched furniture know only too well. This combination is another way to leave a long-distance message without having a close encounter with another cat.

What are you saying when you scratch? The scents on your paws include both your individual smell and also pheromones from the scent glands. Scratching, like urine marking, is often performed along the paths, rather than the far edges, of your hunting range if you spend time outdoors.[24] It is not a 'Keep Out' sign. Scratching along pathways may be a way of making sure you can time-share an area without running into another cat or a sticky-note reminder to yourself. If you live indoors, you may need to scratch more if there is tension between you and other resident cats.[25] If so, this suggests that depositing your own scent in this way is another method of helping you cope. Researchers still do not know exactly what messages are conveyed by the scent from the glands on your paws. The scratching is seen by other cats, but researchers do not know whether you can recognize an individual by the visual pattern of the scratch marks as well as by the scent.

SCENT REASSURANCE

When you are left in a cattery, a loving owner will often leave a familiarly scented object, like a blanket or a bed, with you. Usually, this is an item which will have the family scent and, of course, your own signature scent. Whether or not this familiar scent reassures you has not been fully tested. There is, however, another feline pheromone which helps you feel reassured. This is the scent which was emitted from your mother's skin glands near her nipples, starting three to four days after she gave birth and remaining until two to five days after you were weaned. The message of that odour is one of security, which helps you bond not only with your mother but also with your fellow kittens. This scent keeps the kittens quiet while their mother is away hunting. If they get restless, they might attract predators, as may happen if their mother is away from the nest too long and her maternal scent wears off. So, the reassurance of this particular pheromone may be important for their survival. Research into this pheromone and others has produced synthetic versions of the social odours which are nowadays used to treat household cats suffering from various forms of stress and also to prevent it.

Slowly humans are beginning to appreciate, if not fully understand, the importance of scent in your life and what it means for your happiness.

8

WHAT IT IS LIKE TO FEEL
FELINE EMOTIONS

As a cat, you feel emotions as humans do. Most cat owners have always believed this, and, if asked outside work, most scientists too. They have recognized that, when you run away and hide under the bed, you are feeling fear. Or when you have a noisy fight with a rival neighbouring cat, you are feeling rage. Animal lovers who have seen a mother cat lying so that her kittens can suckle her and washing them when they need it would have little hesitation in believing she is showing the emotion of maternal love. Of course, humans do not always get it right when they decide what emotion a cat is feeling, and that leads to misunderstandings. For example, when you deposit a small amount of urine on your owner's bed. Your owner might believe you are deliberately doing this to get revenge: 'He's doing this to get back at me. He's angry because I punished him for scratching the furniture.' There is another possibility. You may just be urinating because you are suffering from cystitis and have been caught short without time to get to the litter tray, or perhaps you are emotionally frustrated or anxious about something and are scent marking.[1] Your owner thinks you are feeling revengeful anger towards her, because you cannot explain what you are inwardly feeling or what you are physically suffering. She has misunderstood because she cannot ask you what you are feeling.

ANIMAL EMOTIONS

Yet you do have emotions, even if humans cannot always understand them. The problem is that you have no human verbal language to communicate your feelings. You have emotions because as a cat you share much of the same brain design that is common to mammals, including humans. The main difference between your brain and a human brain is that humans have evolved to have a much bigger frontal and especially prefrontal cortex, the front part of the brain that is responsible for much thinking, planning, decision making and pondering. The prefrontal cortex is a regulating part of a brain rather than an emotional part, although the two areas are highly interconnected. You have a relatively smaller prefrontal cortex, compared to the human one, and various areas within it are less developed. The brain networks for emotional processing – that is, subjective feelings – evolved long before sophisticated thinking about these things, and these networks form the basis of what is called the *limbic system*. This part of the brain is common to both cats and humans. As the prefrontal cortex developed later on in evolution, emotional circuits in the limbic system connected with and interacted with some of the higher brain functions in the developing prefrontal cortex. The two are so connected that in both the human and the feline brain they function both from the bottom up, with the emotions of the limbic system affecting thoughts, and from the top down, with the prefrontal cortex able to regulate emotions.[2] Humans, moreover, can use their prefrontal cortex to override their emotional responses and analyse the detail of an emotional situation, but that does not mean they always do.

Emotions are, and have evolved to be, part of the survival mechanism for animals, including humans. Fear, for instance, is a protective emotion and protects us from danger. Without fear you would stroll into the teeth of a terrier that is ready to kill all cats, and without fear a human would cross the road in front of a car and be run down. Without the emotion of maternal care in your feline mother, you would have died as a kitten, and both kittens and occasionally human babies die of neglect if their mother has no maternal feeling. Emotions set the tone for action, influence how you perceive your world and are essential for the propagation and survival of the species, whether feline or human. They are also central to making you an individual, with your own personal preferences and dislikes.

Yet some scientists still say that you and all other cats do not feel emotions. They believe that you are made up of blind instincts, with little, if any, conscious inner life. (Consciousness, even in humans, is notoriously difficult to study scientifically, but being conscious of emotions (feelings) is not the same as having emotional processes. However, some argue the two are inextricably linked.) Some scientists believe that it is anthropomorphic and therefore *per se* unscientific to believe anything else. A bit of relatively recent human history is necessary to explain why cats like you can be still so misjudged by some of the science establishment.

ANIMALS AS MACHINES

The idea that animals do not have emotions is not a new one. Way back in the 17th century the French philosopher René Descartes (1596–1650) argued that, because animals lacked a soul, and as the soul was the basis of human moral thinking, only humans must be conscious. Therefore, other animals could not be conscious. The fearful gasping of a dog trapped in a glass cage from which the air was being removed (one of many unethical experiments on animals at that time) was nothing more than the mechanical reflexes of an automaton, like the creaking of a machine. These reflexes might look like fear and pain, but as the animal did not have feelings, it was argued it could not be experiencing fear or pain.

These ideas were challenged by many, including Charles Darwin (1809–82), in another of his great books, *The Expression of Emotions in Man and Animals* (1872). He looked carefully at the behaviour of the animals in his household – the dogs, the cats and the horses – and tried to come up with some general principles by which emotions in animals and humans might be recognized. He read their emotions by looking at their body language and behaviour. Of your species, cats, he wrote:

> When this animal is threatened by a dog, it arches its back in a surprising manner, erects its hair, opens its mouth and spits. But we are not here concerned with this well-known attitude, expressive of terror combined with anger; we are concerned only with that of rage or anger. This is not often seen but may be observed when two cats are fighting together . . .[3]

Darwin concluded that animals experienced emotions, but subsequent scientists tended to ignore this, with the notable exception at the time of a student named George Romanes (1848–94), a friend of Darwin's, who wrote extensively on animal intelligence.

The prevailing view, however, was that, if you could not prove that animals experienced emotions, then it should be assumed that they did not. Interesting anecdotes about Darwin's family pets or individual animals he had observed were unscientific. The same criticism was applied to Romanes' anecdotes about intelligent animals, based on the principle discussed earlier, Morgan's Canon, which argued we should not assume higher psychological processes are involved if a behaviour can be explained by simpler means.[4] For example, when you urinated on your owner's bed, revengeful anger would be a 'higher psychological process'. Your behaviour should be explained by the 'lowest' motive. Urgent urination due to an illness of the lower urinary tract or an unconscious reflex response to some event would be a 'lower' process that could explain this.

Because nobody could see what was going on in a cat's brain in the first half of the 20th century, scientists concentrated on what they could see and measure – feline behaviour. Behaviourism, the study of the relationship between external environmental events and its consequences only in the form of observable behaviour, was born. A key thought leader in this field was the scientist B F Skinner (1904–90), who researched how rewards and punishments could change behaviour in animals, mostly rats and pigeons. Behaviour which was rewarded (e.g. with food) would be more likely to be repeated by the animal; behaviour which was punished (often by a small electric shock) was likely to be suppressed. Using rewards and punishments, Skinner argued he could even train pigeons how to 'play' football, but they were not truly involved in a game. They simply scored goals to get a food reward as they, like his other animals used in reward experiments, were on starvation rations. All animal behaviour, he contended, was controlled by rewards and punishments. This was the way to change behaviour in both humans and animals. It was not necessary, or indeed even desirable, to discover what, if anything, was going on inside an animal's mind. Thus, strict behaviourists decided it was unscientific to study emotions at all. Only the hard facts of what an animal actually did, its visible behaviour, could be studied.

Skinner went further. As discussed in the Introduction, he maintained that the emotional feelings reported by humans did not exist as a process that shaped behaviour. They were invented by humans who wanted to explain their behaviour. 'The "emotions" are excellent examples of the fictional causes to which we commonly attribute behavior,' he wrote.[5] He did not even consider the possibility that it was the emotional pleasurable anticipation of a reward or the emotional fear of a punishment which might influence how an animal behaved, rather than the reward or punishment itself. In summary, the inside of the minds of his experimental animals was of no interest to him and the absence of proof for animal emotions persuaded him that animal emotions were therefore absent. What mattered was only their visible behaviour. An extreme case of this thinking in the United States involved not just animals but human babies, too young to verbalize pain or fear except by their body language. Because it was felt language was necessary for emotional feelings, the US medical establishment seemed happy to promote the idea that young babies could not have feelings of pain or fear, and as late as the mid-1980s some babies were operated upon without any anaesthetic whatsoever. By contrast in the United Kingdom, it had been illegal to do certain surgical procedures on animals without anaesthesia since 1919.

THE BIRTH OF ETHOLOGY

Around the same time as Skinner, in the first part of the 20th century, ethologists in Europe were studying the outward visible behaviour of animals from a different perspective. They focused on wild animals in their natural environment and also had to concentrate on what they could see – that is, the animal's behaviour. What interested these early ethologists was the innate or instinctive behaviour patterns of a species, rather than the laws governing how an animal learned. Skinner might be training his pigeons to play football in his laboratory, but the ethologists were observing pigeons in the wild and how they behaved in order to survive and thrive. The early ethologists took a different view, and the Dutch Nobel laureate Nikolaas Tinbergen (1907–88) declared (more accurately than Skinner): 'Because subjective phenomena cannot be observed objectively in animals, it is idle to claim or deny their existence.'

Science – and especially scientific funding – is by its nature very cautious, and those wishing to study the emotional lives of animals have often had to keep the very word 'emotion' out of their grant applications.[6] Indeed, one of the pioneers of modern thinking about animal emotion, the Estonian-American neuroscientist Professor Jaak Panksepp (1943–2017), stated, in 2015, 'If you push the frontiers of research you've got to do it in your own time and your own dime'[7] – which is what he did at the beginning of his research. At the time, if 'emotion' was a dirty word in scientific discourse on animals, the word 'consciousness' was even more vehemently shunned.

Advances in technology, however, have changed scientific practice and (to some extent) scientific opinion because we can now look inside the brain to see what is happening using techniques like fMRI (functional magnetic resonance imaging) and PET (positron emission tomography) scans. These technologies mean that what happens in the brain during 'subjective phenomena' can be studied. Your inner experiences, and the inner life of other animals, are no longer a black box. What scientists increasingly see is ever more similarity in brain activity between humans and other mammals, when humans are reporting subjective experiences. The inevitable conclusion, supported by evolutionary argument, has to be that you are not an unthinking, unfeeling machine that only seems to be a thinking feeling being. You experience emotions and, what is more, you are in some way conscious of them. Just because we cannot ask you, as a cat, what your subjective feelings are does not mean you do not have any. You and all cats feel emotions.

What does this growing shift in human scientific attitude mean to you as a cat? If you were in a laboratory, it might mean a great deal, especially in countries that regulate experiments on animals. The scientists in charge have to work out kinder ways of using you in their research. But it also means that your owner is intuitively correct in believing that you have a much more complex inner world, even if they sometimes do not understand which emotions are in play.

Is your inner emotional life the same as that of a human being? Probably not. You may not experience some complicated emotions, but then again, humans might not experience certain cat emotions.

Human self-awareness (a phenomenon scientists call *autonoetic consciousness*) involves the ability to mentally place oneself in the past or future and to examine one's own thoughts, and this seems to be a recent development associated with prefrontal cortical activity. As a cat you may also be free from the complexities of emotions experienced by humans such as shame, guilt, self-loathing and pride, but not all researchers would agree with this.[8] However, many agree now that you do share the more basic emotions with humans. It is even argued that these basic emotions in both humans and cats can be experienced without a neocortex, the more evolved layers of the brain involved in sensory perception, cognition and motor commands.[9]

THE EMOTIONAL NETWORKS

Although scientists may not agree on how many basic emotions there are, they tend to agree that many species have emotional brain networks associated with the following: desire-wanting, frustration-rage, anxiety-fear, lust, care, panic-grief, social affiliation (including the joy of social play) and social repulsion, as well as, of course, pain.[10] Situations giving rise to these emotions do not just rouse brain activity but also trigger other changes in the body such as the release of hormones into the blood and changes in the involuntary nervous system that controls the heart, blood pressure and breathing. These changes, like the parts of the brain that light up with an emotion, can be studied. What both humans and cat experience is often a blend of emotional activity from these primary emotions; this gives their emotional lives a richness like a beautiful painting which is really only made up of a few primary colours. Nonetheless, it is useful to understand the emotional building blocks of your lived experience.

The *desire-wanting* system creates a positive emotion and is a brain network that leads you to seek out many pleasures in life: activities such as feeding, drinking, exploring, hunting and play-hunting with little objects like toy mice. It is a network that makes you get up and go and be curious about the world around you. A good example of desire is when you are hunting mice. Your silent desire and enthusiasm can be read by a human onlooker in the way you are poised to pounce – eyes focused in a hard stare, ears forward, body tense and poised to spring. Hunting is what evolution has designed cats to do in order to get food, and therefore the emotion accompanying it and motivating it is an enthusiastic and pleasurable one. Without the desire to hunt, no feral cat could survive in the countryside. It is common for humans observing you when you are hunting to think that while hunting you are experiencing anger or rage. It is not so. It is a different kind of violence, and different parts of the brain are involved.

Frustration-rage is the negative emotion when you protect what is yours and when you are thwarted or fail to gain a resource you want. When it starts, desire stops. It arises when you are restrained or try to control your territory – indeed, any time your autonomy is challenged.[11] Minor examples of frustration are when your activities are interrupted by a human picking you up or when the door leading to the roast meat on the dining table is shut in your face. Frustration can grow into rage if you are cornered by a threatening dog and, unable to escape, you have to defend yourself by attacking it, or when a hostile neighbouring cat intrudes into your territory. Unlike the poised body and the silent pounce of the hunting cat, you fight with an arched back and ears swivelled back, and with noisy hissing and howling. Your inner emotions of rage when fighting are very different from the positive emotion of hunting, and so are the outward signs of your behaviour.

Fear-anxiety is another negative but protective emotion which is often experienced alongside frustration-rage. Fear-anxiety is a response to a threat to you personally. You will experience it if you feel you are at risk of being harmed. This might be when you are chased away by an angry gardener from the neighbouring allotment, which you have been accustomed to use as a latrine. You will also feel fear-anxiety in the vet's surgery, anticipating that you may soon have a sharp needle jabbed into the scruff of your neck.

The *panic-grief* emotion is the negative emotional response that occurs in relation to social isolation or social loss and which reduces your sense of safety and security. You experience this distress as a kitten if you are isolated from your mother to whom you are tightly bonded. This social pain arises from being a warm-blooded mammal, needing contact with and care from a mother figure. As a kitten you will die unless you are protected and cared for by a mother figure. Panic-grief motivates you to find your mother and is a vital safety and survival emotion. It is the social pain that arises from loss of a social group that protects you from isolation. The extent to which this applies to you as an adult cat is uncertain, despite humans caring for you, because you have the equipment to look after yourself in the form of claws and teeth. You may experience panic-grief when separated from your human owners and familiar surroundings in a boarding cattery, or when you are in a veterinary surgery alone without your normally friendly companion cat. Your individual social pain will depend not only on your individual ability to be sociable but also on your need for safety and security. When your carer is not there, you may experience frustration rather than panic-grief, because you cannot get what you want, when you want it. This can result in you redirecting your frustration into destroying certain things or trigger spraying, perhaps in an attempt to calm yourself down. Some owners might mistake this for signs of panic-grief, when really it is frustration, and what you need is to learn to be not so demanding (and your owner not to be so willing to give you so much for free)!

The *lust* system relates to the positive emotions associated with breeding, but is of little concern to you as a neutered cat. Such is its strength that, if you were an unneutered tomcat, you would leave a comfortable human home for several days or even longer, roaming in search of a mate. It may lead you to chase off other cats or take on fights you might otherwise avoid, in order to increase your chances of having sex. If you are an unspayed female cat, you will also want to get out into the streets and search for a mate. Lust is a great motivator!

Care – nurturing and protecting others – is another generally positive emotion. It is what most mother animals experience when they have young or surrogates for young. Most mammals' survival depends on being cared for in their first days or weeks of life and the actions of caring – suckling, cleaning, warmth providing – can be seen in the behaviour of a mother cat. This is when you provide protection to others, rather than being the one receiving it.

The *social affiliation* emotion that comes from doing things together with friends is a positive one that has intrigued researchers. It includes social play but appears in a brain network that is distinct from the one activated when a cat plays with a toy mouse. Social play is common in kittens but occurs in adults, too. You play properly with another cat when you are both relaxed and safe, and you repeatedly start up another bout of play, which suggests this rough-and-tumble play is very enjoyable. You play with friends, not with enemies. Your rough-and-tumble actions may appear a bit like fighting to a human onlooker, but your claws are retracted, your play bites do not break the skin, and there is no growling or howling. Your play is punctuated with pauses after which both playmates come back for another bout. However, to end play, you might sometimes need to be firm, if your playmate wants to keep going. This does not mean you have fallen out, though. It is important for your owner to appreciate this and not interfere (even with the best of intentions) and make matters worse by telling you off and creating tension with you as a result. What might seem like angry swipe or a nip between cats during play is usually just their way of showing they have had enough.

The opposite of this is the emotion associated with *social repulsion*, which in humans forms the basis of hate. This could be the new kitten that has arrived in your home or simply someone who seems to threaten the comfort of your home. They seem to you to demand far more than they give, and so you may actively reject them.

Pain is also something you share with humans. There is the sharp sensory element of pain when you step on a hot tin roof, but also the emotional aspect. Indeed, this brain network shares many of the features of the network for psychological pain related to grief, and some opioid drugs diminish both physical and psychological pain.[12] Pain will almost always generate unpleasant emotions in you. Tooth pain, for example, which makes humans irritable and anxious about their continuing suffering, will also make you, as a cat, bad tempered and defensive.

HOW EMOTIONS DEVELOP

How does an emotion arise and what happens when it is aroused? We talk about emotions as if they were just inner feelings, but they are much more than that. An emotion can be broken down into five different components – appraisal, automatic physiological reactions, action tendency, behaviour and inner feelings.[13]

An emotion starts with *appraisal* or *assessment*. Suppose you see Fluffy, the cat that lives next door, come into your garden. If you like Fluffy, you will feel a positive emotion. You might want to play with her. If you dislike Fluffy (and maybe have had a stand-off with her or even a fight in the past), you will feel a negative emotion. It all depends on how you assess Fluffy – whether you evaluate her as a friend or a potential threat and whether you assess that you can cope with her presence in your garden. Of course, it might not be Fluffy: it might be an event like a visit to the vet's. You will assess a visit to the vet's as unpleasant, a threat of harm when you feel the pain of an injection. It will strongly get your attention, and your appraisal will be remembered. But events that you ignore, or you do not notice at all, will not be explicitly remembered or arouse a conscious emotion. Not all events carry emotional meaning for you.

This appraisal leads to *automatic physiological reactions* to prepare you for appropriate action, according to your assessment of what is happening. Your heart may beat more rapidly, adrenaline may flood into the bloodstream, and your breathing may become more rapid. If you are experiencing fear, you may begin to sweat in the paw pads of your feet. There will be automatic changes – unconscious reflexes – in your body like your tensing up, or a dry mouth, or eye pupils widening. These involuntary bodily changes often occur more strongly in the negative emotions than in the positive ones.

The third component is when you ready yourself for a particular kind of action, whether it is hiding when the carrier used for the vet visit appears, seeking out and examining the smell in the garden, meowing at the kitchen door or pouncing on that falling leaf. This is your *action tendency* or *motivational tendency*. The relevant emotion will lead you to perform the appropriate types of action. You prepare for what you need to do next, such as run away, stalk towards, or fight. You also communicate your emotional state through your outward behaviour; for example, your ears may part and swivel back to signal you are frustrated. This deliberate expression of emotion – your *behaviour* – is the fourth component, with the fifth being the feelings you generate. Your *inner feelings*, like the feelings of every individual whether cat or human, remain essentially private. Even when a human talks about what they are feeling, other humans cannot know exactly what is being felt. The mystery of other minds stays mysterious.

Breaking down these components of an emotion may give the impression that they happen in a slow and ordered sequence. In fact, usually they are very rapid and seem to come almost at the same time; they also feed back into one another. However, because of all the hormones that are triggered by an emotional response, it can take some time for you to switch your emotional focus. Emotions may be aroused quickly, but the stronger they are, the higher your level of arousal, the more time it will take for you to simmer down. For example, if you are picked up by your human during a fight with another cat, you cannot immediately calm down and while being held by them you may well bite and scratch your rescuer.

MOODS AND TEMPERAMENTS

When an emotional state persists for some time, we tend to call it a *mood*, and moods create an emotional tendency which can set off related emotions more easily. A mood of anxiety may make you more likely to see danger and feel stronger fear. If you are already in an anxious mood, you are more likely to trigger a wide range of negative emotional reactions. A rustle in the undergrowth that is ambiguous to you in a relaxed mood, or even evokes the pleasurable possibility of a mouse, is more likely to be heard as a negative sound, evoking a fear of a predator, when you are in an anxious mood.

Likewise, your *temperament* or personality also creates biases in your emotional reactions. Temperament or personality is your relatively consistent nature which affects the way you interact with the world. Almost every cat owner who has lived with more than one cat knows that each cat has its own individual character. A group of researchers noted as early as 1986: 'We felt that each animal [cat] in our laboratory colony had a distinct personality in the sense that the sum total of its behaviour gave it an identifiable style.'[14] Your individual emotional tendencies may be at least partly due to your genetic make-up, even if it is not predetermined. For example, in this century genetic research has identified a particular gene that functions as a receptor for oxytocin, a hormone and neurotransmitter associated with social relationship that some call the *love hormone*. In dogs, differing forms of this gene affect their friendliness towards familiar and strange humans, and now researchers have found three different forms of this gene (alleles) in cats.[15] One of these seems to be clearly associated with what the researchers called roughness, a trait that suggested the individual cat was irritable, dominant, forceful and moody.

Your emotional life, not unlike the emotional life of your fellow mammal *Homo sapiens*, influences and enriches your feline world. It is not unconscious and instinctive; you can control how you respond to things. If you experience pain and fear having been stung by a bee that you were prodding with your paw, you will encode this as a memory and in future you will no longer consider that bees are a kind of flying toy. You will now appraise and assess them as potentially painful.[16] You have learned this. After all, you have both feeling and thinking (cognition) going on in your brain. Your emotions are modified and shaped by the thinking part of your brain and, conversely, without emotions you would not be motivated to remember and learn.[17] True, you do not have the cognitive powers of a human, but you are not mindless. You can and do think, so this is what we turn to in the next chapter.

9

WHAT IT IS LIKE TO THINK AS A CAT

You do not think like a human, but that does not make you mindless. You do not think like a dog or a horse. You think like a cat, because you experience the world like a cat. Your mind is adapted from evolution to think in a way which helps you survive and thrive as a cat. Of course, humans cannot ask you what you are thinking. So, it is difficult to know what is going on in your mind and humans can only make informed guesses about what you are thinking during your daily life.

And what does 'thinking' mean? Researchers consider it a form of what they call *cognition*. The scientific definition, which we are using in this chapter when we write 'thinking', is 'information processing in the broadest sense, from gathering information through the senses to making decisions and performing appropriate actions, regardless of the complexity of any internal representational processes that behaviour might imply'.[1] A cat that cannot think like a cat does not survive in the wild. And a human who thought like a cat would definitely not be able to do much scientific research! Every species thinks like whichever species it is, so making comparisons between you and a human in things like intelligence is not very useful.[2]

Nor it is helpful to assume that you are stupid, just because you do not think like a human. You are simply different and adapted to a different lifestyle. Nevertheless, a lot of human researchers have put a lot of energy into trying to discover if in at least some ways other animals think like humans. So, they have concentrated on things like language, reasoning, tool use and something called *theory of mind* (the ability to attribute mental states to others). Most of this research has been done on apes and monkeys, some has been done on dogs, but very little on cats. Dogs and primates are easier to test in the laboratory, but some of the tests have been so human centred in their design that it is not surprising that the animals being tested acted like 'dumb beasts'.

FAULTY INVESTIGATIONS

Researchers have sometimes used poor test design for cats when studying the concept of *object permanence* – that is, if an object is no longer visible, do you realize it still exists? Common sense suggests that you should know that an invisible object still exists. If a mouse disappears into its mousehole, you will wait outside the hole for it to reappear, then pounce on it. Sometimes you will wait a very long time. If you thought it no longer existed when it disappeared into its mousehole, why would you wait? Yet some human researchers have claimed otherwise on the basis of their tests. If an object is hidden in a container and moved behind a screen, where the container is emptied out of sight, is it of any interest to you?[3] It should not be surprising that cats involved in such a task lose interest and don't seem to understand what has happened. But this does not mean that cats think the object has just disappeared into thin air nor does it make them dumb; it is just a meaningless test from your perspective. In a better-designed version of the test, described as 'ecologically relevant' and held in a human home, cats performed much better.[4] However, even in this version the researchers noted the occasional lack of feline cooperation. Some of the cats just walked away before or during the investigation!

In other laboratory studies, ill-thought-out tests have resulted in cats appearing less competent than pigeons. For example, cats like you have been much less successful in pressing a lever in order to obtain food, while pigeons learn to do this without much problem. But perhaps 'cats are not well adapted to learning a monotonous task that involves repeated pressing of a lever in order to obtain food,' as Patrick Bateson and Dennis C Turner suggest in *The Domestic Cat: The Biology of Its Behaviour*.[5] Another example of inappropriate investigation came from one of the first psychology researchers, the American Edward Thorndike (1874–1949), in 1911.[6] He concluded that cats cannot learn by imitating each other, a form of social learning. He put two cats into a box divided by see-through wooden bars, where the learner cat could watch a demonstrator cat successfully open the latch mechanism of the box by pulling a string. The learner cat wanted to escape but failed to learn how to do this by watching the demonstrator. Thorndike concluded that cats could not learn by imitation, but we know from subsequent research that kittens can learn from watching their mother. Indeed, even a non-social reptile, a tortoise, can learn from watching another tortoise successfully solve a detour task. Thorndike was putting his cats into an unnatural situation that did not set them up for learning from another. Cats do not use others to help them escape. If the learner cat was stressed by confinement, why should it focus on a solution from an unfamiliar demonstrator cat, whose proximity might also add to the stress of the situation? Cats like you usually avoid strange cats or cats with whom you do not have a friendly relationship. Thorndike's conclusions were invalid because he did not take account of the nature of a cat and how it impacts learning. This is precisely the problem with behaviourist scientists who do not think about what is going on inside the animal's head.

A major problem which acts against cats like you showing your intelligence in human tests is a relative lack of motivation. While dogs are eager to co-operate with human tests, you are often less willing to make the effort. Dogs spend enormous amounts of effort observing exactly what their human owners are doing. As social animals, they are always checking in on their social companions, ready to co-operate with them. As a more independent animal, you are less interested in your owners and therefore pay less attention to them. It has been argued by some that the more social an animal is, the more complex will be its mental life – the *social intelligence hypothesis*. According to this idea, tests on relatively less sociable cats will show that they are less mentally developed than dogs. But cats, while they do not co-operate in hunting activities, do co-operate in raising their kittens, sharing nursing and kitten-sitting duties. They also collectively move their nest sites. Filip Jaroš, a Czech researcher, has argued that this nest-moving behaviour in feral cats shows that cats 'have cognitive abilities to share attention, truly cooperate and constitute shared meanings'.[7]

These are complex mental abilities that need further careful investigation.

A DIFFERENT KIND OF INTELLIGENCE

Human judgement of your mental abilities may also be affected by a longstanding bias relating to the human mind. The idea that humans are rational beings goes back in history to the Stoic philosophers of the 3rd century BCE or earlier, and became embedded in Christianity via Augustine of Hippo (354–439 CE), who legitimized eating meat on the grounds that, 'it is not given to them [animals] to have reason in common with us'.[8] Scientists studying animal cognition rarely remind people that a lot of human thinking is not careful logical reasoning, but quick decisions based on emotion or rule of thumb. Indeed, complex human activities, such as driving a car, can be performed without much conscious thought at all, if the driver knows the route and is busy listening to the radio. The human mind is capable of logical reasoning but not permanently engaged in conscious logical reasoning. Most of the time, like other species, it is simply trying to develop and confirm its expectations.

Language is a useful subject for considering the complexities of the feline mind – assuming you do not adopt a definition of language that depends on words. Much effort was made by some scientists to train apes to speak using human language before it was realized they do not have the vocal capacity of humans. However, when training them to use hand gestures (sign language) or key presses instead of human words, they have appeared to communicate much more than expected. Verbal language comes naturally to humans but not to other animals. As a cat you do not have the equivalent of words which can be assembled and reassembled in different ways. You have a language of vocal sounds, body positions, scent messages and touch communication, but these signals have only relatively simple meanings compared with words. They are signals that can identify the sender and express messages like 'I was here', 'Ready to mate' or 'Notice me'. Or so it is thought. However, female cats sharing kitten duties and collectively moving kitten nests may be involved in some form of mental co-ordination, which may require communication between all the mothers. If so, something quite complex is going on between the cats.[9] The more we humans study these phenomena with an open mind, the more complex and sophisticated we realize they are. At the moment scientists have not studied cat-to-cat communication well enough to be sure it is only limited and simple.

However, when it comes to words, you can recognize several individual human words that are important to you – which is one reason why you may go and hide under the bed if you hear the 'vet' word! These words are associated in your mind with significant results: they mean something might happen which you need to know about. You recognize your own name, for example, because when the word for your name is uttered, it may be followed by pleasant or unpleasant consequences. It is therefore a sound worth paying attention to. Four Japanese researchers confirmed this with an ingenious series of simple experiments.[10] Cats that were in their own homes, living on their own or with only a few other cats, were tested to see if they could recognize their own name from four other words, general nouns with the same length and accent to their name word, all spoken by their owners. Cats living with four or more cats in the same household and cats living in a cat café were tested in the same way, then given another test to see if they recognized their own name, as opposed to the names of the other cats. Some of the same researchers had previously discovered that most cats could recognize their owner's voice from the voices of strangers.[11] So, they also tested the cats to see if they could recognize their name from other words, even when their name was uttered by an unfamiliar person. Most of the cats living in a household responded to their own name by moving their ears or head towards the sound, even if their name was uttered by a stranger. Their own name got their attention. The researchers concluded: 'This implies that cats' names can be associated with rewards such as food, petting and play, or with punishments such as taking them to a veterinary clinic or to a bath.'[12] The name words got feline attention, but most of the cats did not respond back with a meow or a tail-up signal – that is, the name recognition did not prompt a 'conversation', as it might do with a fellow human, merely attention. Also, the cats that lived in a multi-cat household were as likely to respond to the names of the co-resident cats as to their own. The café cats, however, living in an environment with many humans coming and going – where there is possibly indiscriminate petting – did not respond.

So, responding to your name may mean that you just learned to associate it with its consequences, rather than recognizing it as a specific label referring to you as an individual. In other words, you recognize your name but probably do not understand that your name is a word for your identity. Building a concept that a particular sound is associated with your personal identity is not the way you think. Identifying the inner self with a name word is something that the human mind does, but your cat mind does not need such concepts. What the name experiments show for sure, however, is that you can learn from experience. If the 'vet' sound precedes a veterinary visit, after a few occasions of an unpleasant consequence, you will run and hide when you hear it. In your mind, you have associated the 'vet' word with its consequences. However, in a further study, cats could also link the name of a familiar human or the human-given name of a co-resident cat with photographs of their faces. They matched the name to the face. 'A remaining question is how cats learn names,' concluded the researchers.[13]

CAT LESSONS – LEARNING AND TRAINING

You can learn many other things that are important to you during your life. Take the hunting instinct. You have an innate tendency to hunt small moving objects like mice and to do this you perform a sequence of behaviours. First you hear and see the prey, then you stalk it, then you pounce on it, grab it with paws or mouth, and finally eat it. This particular sequence is relatively hard-wired into you. When you are playing with a mouse, you do not complete the sequence because you are not hungry. You play with it, performing parts of this sequence, often in order – pouncing before grabbing rather than just grabbing the corpse in front of you. You learn to modify this sequence in other ways when required. If you kill bats or birds in the air, you have learned to leap upwards rather than pounce downwards and to bat these animals to the ground where they can be more easily grabbed. If you live in a rural area with good hunting opportunities, you will also have learned to modify your pounce in long grass. Instead of merely pouncing by rising on your back legs and propelling yourself forwards with your forelegs, the normal pounce, you will do a leap into the air with all four feet off the ground, in order to clear the high foliage. The hunting instinct is a tendency (not a fixed behaviour sequence) that is hard-wired into you as the language-development instinct is hard-wired into humans, but your mind can learn from results and modify it. Do you logically reason out the mouse's position before each pounce? No, you don't. But neither do human car drivers use rational logic when they react fast and routinely switch motorway lanes to avoid a collision. The mental process before these fast decisions, whether in human driving or in feline hunting, does not need to be conscious, since such complex thinking would slow the process down and could cost you dearly. Your brain makes the behavioural choice, and sometimes it might tell you about it afterwards.

Your ability to learn has been tested in experiments. Scientists love mazes for animal testing, so it is not surprising that cats have been trained to use a maze.[14] This was a T-shaped maze, where a food reward was placed in one of the two ends. The researchers made efforts to make sure the cats had got used to the maze before the testing started, and that they had positive experiences with the people doing the testing. After that, the cats learned that the reward was on one side, then, after they had become proficient in getting to the reward fast, it was placed on the other side. This took them a bit longer to learn, but they did so without too much difficulty. There was one snag, a difficulty that occurs in almost all cat training. Every now and again a cat would fail to concentrate on what it was meant to be doing. This behaviour did not seem to be due to fear, because the cats had been trained to get used to the maze before the testing started. Nor did it seem to be due to any outside distraction such as noise. 'We were unable to identify any environmental and behavioural phenomena to explain this inconsistency,' the researchers admitted.[15]

If you had been doing this maze test, might you simply have become bored with the maze, or maybe the food reward was not good enough to motivate you? Cats like you enjoy investigating and learning about your wider environment, which is why you need plenty of activities in your home life. You have an enormous curiosity driven by your own interests rather than those around you. However, that does not mean you cannot be trained to do things others find interesting.

A sensational example of cat training was the feline performances staged by Antony Hippisley Coxe (1912–88), who ran a circus act of four or five cats in the 1950s. Celia saw these in 1953 and remembers how the cats performed their tricks with a slow dignity. 'Fear and pain are unknown quantities which need never be used in training domestic animals,' Coxe wrote in his book about his circus experiences. The only time he gave a small slap to a cat, it refused to perform for four whole days.[16] Unlike dogs, which (alas for them) accept punishment from cruel trainers, domestic cats simply run away and avoid the individual in future. Punishment-free training is a must for cats. A more modern example of impressive cat training is Dominique and His Flying House Cats, a feline troupe based in Florida that can be seen on YouTube. Dominique LeFort's cats perform in the open air, without the confinement of a theatre or a circus ring. They could simply jump down and disappear into the crowd any time if they were not enjoying it. Instead, they leap from high chair to high chair, jumping over Dominique and also through hoops. These are exceptional examples of cat training, and whatever the ethical implications of public animal performances, they highlight how individual cats can be trained to a high level of performance if properly motivated. You, like most cats, have enormous potential, if only your human took time to discover what really motivates you.

What does your ability to be trained by a human mean for you? Your life could be improved if your owner did some simple reward training. The cat carrier is associated in your mind with the potentially horrible trip to the vet, and your owner probably bundles you somewhat roughly into it. However, this would be far less stressful for you if you were trained by tasty treats to go into it willingly. There are now several manuals for this sort of training, including *The Trainable Cat: How to Make Life Happier for You and Your Cat*.[17] If you are an indoor cat without much activity, a few simple training tricks could be fun for both you and your owner, especially if you are an indoor-only cat. Reward training like this arouses the pleasurable emotion of anticipatory desire, so much so that most cats purr as they perform.

FELINE MEMORY

What cat training also shows is that you have a perfectly good memory. Indeed, you are learning all the time without any special training by humans. You learn that if you sit between your owner and the computer, they will give you attention and probably a few strokes (a pleasurable tactile reward) before removing you. You learn that a meow gets your owners' attention. You learn that if you roll on your back, your owner is likely, if you enjoy it, to tickle your belly. Attention and strokes are pleasurable and create pleasurable emotions in you. What is rewarding gets repeated. If you get these rewards after the first time you act this way, you are more likely to do the same actions again. This is the way you learn – from consequences – and you need a memory for this learning to occur. Owners also learn by consequences and do not tickle the belly of cats that dislike it!

Two kinds of memory investigated in cats are described as *working memory* and *long-term memory*.[18] Working memory is what you use to attend to and perform specific actions from moment to moment. Working memory is important for tasks like object permanence, as it tests how long you can keep a now-invisible object in your mind. Humans use working memory when reading this chapter, for instance, as they are taking in the meaning of the words and putting them into the context of the paragraph. The time this information stays in the human mind has been variously estimated as 15 seconds to 10 minutes. Tests have suggested that your working memory is often less than 30 seconds to perhaps a minute long, but clearly you can wait for prey for much longer. For training tasks, you will remain focused only for these shorter times and sometimes much less, which explains why good trainers reward their dogs and cats quickly after the desired action and keep sessions short. Your long-term memory is far better. Nobody has studied whether you can retain a memory for life, as humans can, but in various tests cats that have learned something visually or through hearing can clearly remember it ten to twenty minutes later, and odour memory can definitely last many months.[19]

You can also work out where your owner is standing from hearing their voice when they are out of sight – so-called *mental mapping*. But can you do mental time travel? You can clearly make simple predictions about the future, but can you think back to an episode in the past and recreate it in your mind? Or think forwards and use the idea of a future event to plan for the future? Humans simply do not know if you can do these sorts of things, although the tests on pigeons, scrub jays and monkeys suggest that in a limited way animals may be able to time-travel in their minds. This idea is still very controversial, however.[20] Even if you remember the past or imagine the future, it may be in a very different way to the way that human minds work.

You are able to keep track of time intervals, becoming demanding when it is time for your regular dinner. Although this might be thought to suggest some idea of mental time travel, it is far more likely to be simply a response to internal bodily changes causing hunger urges. It is worth pausing here to note that you may experience time quite differently from humans. A seven-year-old cat is supposedly physiologically the 'same' age as a 44-year-old human because your feline body ages more quickly than the human body. But your lifespan may not feel faster or shorter to you. It may feel as long to you as a human lifespan feels to a human.[21] Your shorter lifespan therefore may also explain the shortness of your working memory compared to adult humans. Your 30 seconds of working memory may take as much effort and be experienced by you as more like the human working memory of 10 minutes. It does not seem to you that you are living in the fast lane, but instead that humans are living in the slow lane: a slow lane like the way a sloth's lifestyle appears to a human.

INDICATORS OF INTELLIGENCE

Tool use is another way that humans have judged the intelligence of animals, but this has not yet been reported in cats (although the definition of a tool seems to be becoming increasingly vague). Indeed, it would be difficult for you to use a tool with your paws, and it would be equally difficult to use a tool with your mouth. Cats can carry prey or kittens with their mouth, but this is usually straightforward transportation from one place to another. At the beginning of the 20th century, it was thought that humans were the only animals to use tools, but now tool use has been seen in chimpanzees, Caledonian crows and other birds, and something a little like tool use has even been seen in ants. *Aphaenogaster* worker ants transport liquid food back to the nest by soaking up the liquid in debris, making food-soaked tools which they then carry back to the nest.[22] The use of tools is not therefore a simple indicator of sophisticated intelligence requiring a complex brain.

Another attempt to test cat intelligence was to see if you can count or, rather, if you can distinguish a small from a large quantity. Cats like you do not count up to ten, like most adult humans (some indigenous Amazonians simply have a few numbers, then consider everything else 'many'), but you can distinguish between two dots and three dots in order to obtain food. The cats tested in this way had to learn this, rather than spontaneously knowing it, possibly partly because static dots did not readily get their attention. The cats involved were not numerate but instead identified the larger number of dots by the larger area they took up rather than by counting them.[23] This method of distinguishing quantities without counting is also found in human babies, apes, monkeys and fish. You do not need to count, but it makes evolutionary sense that, all other things being equal, you can choose a larger bit of food over a smaller one.

Perhaps the holy grail of intelligence is the ability to have *theory of mind* – whether you can imagine what is going on in the mind of another person or cat. If you run away from an angry, shouting human, is this just because you have associated human shouting with potential punishing consequences? Or do you read that shouting human's mind and conclude that he is thinking about harming you? This latter alternative, the ability to attribute a mental state to another being, is what is meant by having a theory of mind. Many research hours have been spent trying to design studies to test this. For example, can an animal understand what another animal perceives, predict what that animal will understand, and then go on to mislead the other animal by deception? Dogs have been tested for this ability in a wide variety of ways, as have chimpanzees, goats, horses, various birds and even pigs. The interpretation of results is still controversial, and these tests have not proved conclusively that any of these animals have the mental ability to imagine, to any great extent, what another animal or human is thinking. Dogs that are tuned into human behaviour can learn to respond differently to humans who habitually deceive them about the location of food. But these talents could involve relatively simple learning, based on excellent canine observation of human behaviour, rather than the ability to assess what another being is thinking. Indeed, work with dogs indicates they may be more interested in reading a human's emotion than their motivation, which may have served them well in the long evolution alongside people. There is evidence that you too can recognize emotions in humans, but this also is not the same as being able to attribute thoughts to a human being and does not add up to theory of mind.[24] Perhaps because of the difficulty of testing cats like you in a laboratory, so far there has been no theory of mind investigation into cats.

Another strand of investigation of these higher forms of cognition aims to see if animals recognize themselves in a mirror, an ability which might suggest that they are self-aware. The classic test consists of putting a mark on the animal's body and seeing if, in front of a mirror, that animal touches the mark to explore it. Elephants, apes and some birds do seem to recognize that the mirror image is of themselves, but cats have not been tested in this way. You have never had to learn the potential value of a mirror. You greet your own reflection as if it was an intruder rather than your own self-image, or you simply ignore the image because you have learned it is of no great interest to you. You tune it out in the same way that you have learned to ignore pictures on TV. However, it is controversial whether or how far this particular mirror test proves that the animal has a concept of its individual selfhood.[25] Is a mirror image the right way to test for self-concept? Should a cat like you be tested using a scent mark, rather than a mirror mark? A scent mark might be far more relevant to you, as a cat, than a mirror mark, and an olfactory mirror has been used to test dogs, which typically fail the visual mirror test.

'NOT LIKE US – LIKE US – NOT LIKE US'

You think but not like humans think. We get back to this truth. Perhaps the easiest way to appreciate some of the differences between humans and cats is the image of a three-layered 'similarity sandwich' developed by the British-Australian ethologist Clive Wynne in his book *Do Animals Think?*[26] The three layers of the sandwich are 'not like us – like us – not like us'. The bottom layer of the sandwich is made up of your different senses – your amazing sense of smell, your lack of strong colour vision, your acute hearing of ultrasonic noises, your lack of taste for sweetness, and your amazingly tactile whiskers. You are not like a human at the bottom layer. The middle layer of the sandwich is that you have a memory, you can learn from experience, you can choose an appropriate action from experience, you can communicate with others of your own species, and you have a sense of quantity and time. These abilities you have in common with humans. At the top of the sandwich are the human abilities that you do not have and do not need – language with words and grammar, tool use and theory of mind. As Professor Wynne writes: 'Every animal's world is different, just as every animal's lifestyle and niche are different. And yet there are also commonalities in animal minds, because we are all living on the same planet and descended from the same slimy ancestors.'[27]

The mystery of your feline mind has been probed but we still have a lot to learn. However, if humans can think more like you, and see things from your perspective as a cat and as an individual, there is less risk of the misunderstanding and problems that can result in you losing your human home.

10

WHAT IT IS LIKE BEING A RESCUE CAT

I t's easy to stray from home if a cat flap allows you to come and go at will. You may run off and get lost; you may be abandoned by a human who is moving house; or you may decide to leave a home which is too stressful for you. You will then join the shifting population of unowned cats, a population which is continually being increased by litters of kittens or by strays like you joining. It is a population also being continually decreased by traffic accidents, diseases and cat rescuers. The rescuers may be rescue organization trappers or just individuals who give a home to a cat that turns up in their garden. It is a rolling homeless population whose basic numbers largely depend on the amount of food and shelter available. In the United Kingdom, for example, you will be joining more than a quarter of a million cats living outside human households.[1] This figure only includes cats within urban areas, so the total figure is certainly much higher, despite years of neutering campaigns for both owned and unowned cats in that country. There are also a further estimated 130,000 cats passing through UK rescue charities during a year.[2] In many other countries the figures are much higher. There are 4.9 million pet cats in Australia and about 700,000 strays living in urban areas.[3] It is estimated there that, depending on rainfall, there may be as many as 5.6 million feral cats living wild in the bush – more than the total number of pet cats.[4] In the USA, there are about 58 million pet cats[5] and an estimated 30–40 million living on the streets or living independently from humans.[6] So, if the estimate of unowned cats outside UK households is correct, perhaps at least one in twenty of the cat population is either living rough or in a cat rescue establishment. In many other countries the proportion is much higher. One estimate suggests that only half the 600 million cats in the world live as pets in a house.[7] That leaves a lot of cats living on the street or surviving in the countryside in just about every country of the world. This may lead some to question whether the cat has ever really been domesticated. However, there are clear differences in your behaviour and that of your wild cousins, and there is also enormous variation in the lifestyles of domestic cats.

The International Society for Feline Medicine (ISFM) has categorized unowned cats into three different groups: feral cats, street or community cats, and stray pet cats.[8] This is a kind of spectrum ranging from completely wild or feral cats surviving on their own without human help, through to community cats without owners but with some human help, through to pet cats that have lost their home and now live on their wits. Your lifestyle will vary according to which group you belong to.

OUT IN THE WILD

In the first category are the independent *feral cats* that survive without any help from or contact with humans. If there is enough food and shelter, these cats will live in groups of related females with visits from males, which have a wider range. They will chase outsiders out of their core territory, often a barn or a deserted building, but share overlapping hunting ranges with cats from other groups. Males come and go, visiting the females. Within the group, if you are part of it, you will also have special friends, or *preferred associates* – the term researchers prefer. With these favoured cat friends, you will be in close contact, grooming each other and perhaps in good times even playing together as adults. This life independent of humans may be shorter than the life of a pampered pet, but it is fully lived with lots of opportunities to do what you as a cat enjoy – sex, kittens, hunting and more hunting. These cats are not generally suitable for a human home and so should not be 'rescued' from their independent life.

If you are a feral cat in Australia, where some have blamed feral cats for the decline of a hundred or so native species including such rare marsupials as the bilby, bandicoot, bettong and numbat, your future may be grim.[9] Shooting and trapping are now the basis of trying to eliminate feral cats in Australia, but in the past less humane and less efficient methods – both in Australia and elsewhere – have included poisoned baits, gassing and even the introduction of specific cat diseases. A more humane method of getting rid of feral cats, if land is going to be developed or if their numbers have got too high, is to trap them and then euthanize them.[10] However, the problem even with lethal methods is that a population soon returns to fill the vacant space. Leave just one pregnant female (and there always seems to be at least one cat that evades trappers) and within months the population is beginning to climb again. Even if every single cat is killed, feral or stray cats from neighbouring areas will move into the vacant space. Lethal methods of control are not efficient. Only on islands or in fenced-off regions does the lethal destruction of feral cats stand a chance of producing a cat-free environment – albeit one that may then have an excessive number of rats and/or rabbits, both of which can be harmful in a different way to native species. In contrast to cat eradicators are the many cat trappers who want to help the cats they trap. These, and many cat feeders who put out food for unowned cats, feel a strong bond with stray cats like you. Indeed, in some European cities the killing of stray cats is forbidden.[11]

If you are a feral cat, the best outcome for you is to be part of a Trap, Neuter and Return, or TNR, programme (sometimes the 'R' stands for Relocate, if the original territory is not available). In these programmes, healthy feral or community cats are neutered, then returned to their territory or a similar one. Diseased cats are euthanized, domestic strays are put up for adoption, and kittens young enough to be socialized to humans are adopted out as pets. If the original territory is not available, the feral cats are relocated somewhere suitable such as stables or farms, where their pest-control activities are useful to the owners. Most TNR programmes appoint a volunteer whose role is to feed the cats regularly and report back if any new stray animals enter the territory. New arrivals are then in turn trapped, neutered and either returned or adopted out. Without this continued supervision and neutering, populations usually build up again. TNR schemes that do not feed the returned cats have been criticized as being inhumane and called by some 'Trap, Neuter and Starve' schemes. However, in areas where feral cats have successfully survived by hunting without human help, if you are returned without regular feeding, you may survive reasonably well, and all the better for having been neutered.

If you are lucky enough, as a feral cat, to join a good TNR programme, your life will be longer and better than if there had been no human intervention. Barring accidents, you may lead a reasonably long and healthy life and you will enjoying a rich outdoor life. One of the longest-running, best-organized TNR programmes, which took place in a waterfront Massachusetts town, was reviewed by two researchers.[12] A third of the cats that were trapped turned out to be sociable and were adopted; the rest were feral or community cats that were neutered, vaccinated and returned to the waterfront. It took two and a half years to trap and neuter all the original cats. After they had been returned there was 'a steady improvement' in their general health, in part due to the regular feeding by volunteers, in part due to neutering. The neutered males were less likely to suffer injury and illness from fighting, while the females were relieved from the burden of continual kitten bearing. Because incoming cats were monitored and either neutered and returned, or adopted out, the population dropped steadily despite the longer lives led by the cats involved. After six years the population was kitten free, and after a further eleven years the cat population dropped from three hundred to zero at the death of the last cat, named Zorro, living on the territory.

CAT SANCTUARIES – A FATE WORSE THAN DEATH?

If you are less fortunate as a feral, you may be trapped and then confined. There are still cat 'sanctuaries' where you may have to live out the rest of your life away from your free-to-roam lifestyle. In the better sanctuaries, you will live in a large, well-designed enclosure with other, unrelated feral cats without any attempt at taming. Some of these cat sanctuaries, however, have relatively barren enclosures with a large number of cats. One such shelter, the subject of a sociological study in the United States covering the period 1996–2000, consisted of five small rooms of the first floor of a two-family house with an enclosed back porch.[13] While there was an isolation room and pens for new residents, there were nevertheless 50–60 stray and feral cats, some waiting for adoption, as well as other long-stay residents living 'free' in three small rooms and the porch. Although most of the feline inmates showed 'social cohesion' and had 'preferred associates', or cat friends, a few individuals showed continued aggression towards other cats. Some humans consider long confinement of this kind a satisfactory trade-off for regular meals and safety from accidents, but if you are unlucky enough to be a natural loner, would you agree? The presence of many unrelated adult cats in such close quarters might be very stressful for you, particularly if the population is not stable.

The worst outcome for you will be a sanctuary where feral cats are confined in pens and 'tamed'. This is less common now that TNR is widely recommended, but still occurs occasionally. Dr Lauren Finka, cat-welfare scientist and author of *The Cat Personality Test*, declares:

It is not advisable to ever try to force a cat to accept contact and proximity to people against their will, especially if they are highly stressed or fearful during the process. This means that the standard practices of trying to 'tame' cats (of any age), where the cat is fearful and distressed, but cannot avoid human contact, should be avoided. These methods are not compatible with good cat welfare, and they are very unlikely to lead to a change in the cat's temperament, where the cat develops generalized sociability to humans. As a result, these cats tend to struggle living in the typical domestic home and may not meet an owner's needs or expectations of a cat–human relationship.[14]

In these circumstances you may be worse off emotionally, if not physically, than you were when living without human help. 'The emphasis is on rescue and keeping cats safe,' says Vicky Halls, project manager for cat-friendly homing at International Cat Care. 'But rescuing cats is not an end in itself. It's only a means to an end.'[15]

A HALFWAY HOUSE

The next category consists of the *street cats* or *community cats*, a category with a status somewhere between wild and household pet. In urban areas, many of those born without close human contact will nevertheless have some contact with humans later in their lives, often with cat lovers who feed their local unowned cats. A few of these cats might become house cats if a regular feeder invites them into the household for several months, but very few would ever become cuddle cats and they would probably be miserably unhappy if kept as indoor-only cats. Moreover, it is often impossible for the rescuers to know how far the cats they trap are socialized to humans. It is very difficult to distinguish between the partly socialized street cats and those that are just strays that once had a home. 'You can't tell in advance,' explains Lis Wells, who has been trapping cats for more than 30 years for various UK cat-rescue charities. 'Cats that have been out on the streets for some time often get labelled as feral when they are not.'[16]

If you are lucky, your cat rescuers will not label you too quickly but will treat you as an individual. The wrong label may lead to a long and unhappy residence in a cat shelter, where your level of stress and your apparent 'unfriendly' behaviour make you unlikely to be adopted. Even if you are not fully feral, entering a TNR programme with feeders may be a far better option than attempts to find you a pet home. And if you are a community cat that must be moved from where you are living, you can be homed to stables, farms or market gardens, where you can be cared for and fed by humans at a safe (for you) distance. International Cat Care calls cats in this position *inbetweeners*.[17] They may be the most difficult cats to place in the right environment. There are only a few adopters or fosterers willing to take on cats that do not want contact with their human. Most people desire to adopt cats that are friendly and happy,[18] and if you are one of these inbetweeners, you are not going to be happy with too much human attention.

CAT-FRIENDLY HOMING

These post-rescue decisions are difficult ones for cat lovers trying to do the right thing by you. Of course, if you are a pet cat surviving outside a human household for the first time for only a few months, you will usually make a relaxed and happy pet if adopted. As a homeless pet cat, you can sometimes survive for years if you can find someone to feed you. Forbes, a tabby-and-white pet cat from Aberdeen in Scotland, went missing in 2011 but was picked up by the Scottish Society for Prevention of Cruelty to Animals (SSPCA) ten years later only two miles from his original home.[19] He was thin but otherwise healthy at the age of 12. His human family were tracked down because he had been microchipped. They were delighted to get him back.

The worst fate of all for you is to be rescued by a dysfunctional charity, only to live in worse conditions than when you were on the street. In 2013 owners of a registered 'rescue' charity in Oxfordshire were jailed for animal neglect, after the Royal Society for Prevention of Cruelty to Animals (RSPCA) seized 78 domestic animals including horses, cats, dogs and goats that were living in unacceptable conditions.[20] The judge described the charity as 'a rescue centre from which animals needed to be rescued'. There are also well-meaning but cat-addicted individuals who fill their house with cats but do not have the money or space for proper care or vets' bills. Being shut up in a house crowded with diseased or stressed cats is a far worse life than the life on the streets. Indeed, it is one of the principles of cat-friendly homing, according to International Cat Care, that no cat should be worse off as a result of human intervention. 'What worried me most of all when I visited cat shelters at the start of the cat-friendly homing project,' says Vicky Halls of International Cat Care, 'was hearing the carers saying, "He's been there for six months but nobody wants him." '[21]

The principles of this cat-friendly homing project are the following:

- Only cats suitable for a human home should go through the pet 'homing' process.
- Cats should spend as little time as possible in homing centres.
- No cat should be worse off as a result of human intervention.
- Confinement should not be prolonged or permanent.
- Each cat should be treated as an individual.
- All cats and kittens should be neutered at the earliest opportunity.[22]

Nowadays many large rescue organizations are aware of the need to quarantine newcomers and have good premises with isolation units. Without quarantine, with barren housing and long stays before adoption, upper respiratory infections and various viruses flourish.[23] Indeed, the longer you stay in a rescue shelter the more likely you are to get sick. So, what kind of cat rescue would give you the best chance of finding a new and loving home fast? If you are lucky enough to be rescued by a good charity, you will be housed in a single pen with outdoor access and without the visual sight of other cats. If you are unlucky, you will be housed after rescue in a small, barren metal cage, which prioritizes hygiene over your emotional well-being. In some places, you may even be housed in a group with previously unfamiliar cats, rather than in a single pen or in a foster home. Better-organized rescues, which still group-house cats, keep the groups down to four to six individuals, and rehome all of the cats before starting a new group. But if you are unlucky, you may be housed in a group where frequent changes owing to cats leaving and arriving maximize your stress, which will play an important part in making you vulnerable to disease. From your point of view, better housing makes you happier and healthier in rescue. From a human rescuer point of view, better housing and quicker adoptions literally pay off, with shorter stays and lower vet bills compensating for the greater space and cost needed by better housing. This allows more cats to be rescued. Sadly, many animal-rescue charities do not have the time and energy to reflect on this.

SETTLING IN

The first two or three days in a rescue shelter are usually intensely stressful for you. You may have been trapped and transported by car in the trap to the shelter. There you are handled by strange humans and placed in a pen that smells of cleaning fluids in an unknown environment that smells of strange cats. You may even be able to see the next-door strange cat through the barriers of the cage – a sight which is threatening to a non-sociable cat. The scent profile of a cat shelter is quite unlike anything in your previous life, as are its noises. A well-designed pen will have somewhere you can hide; a badly designed one will mean that you have to huddle against a corner or try to burrow underneath the blanket which is there for a bed. In a small cage, the litter tray is close to your bedding and to the food bowl, something that no cats like. There are no perching places and no privacy. Worse still, if it is a general animal rescue, there may be the scent and noise of nearby dogs. There may also be loud unfamiliar noises – people talking, a washing machine in use, and the clatter of cat bowls when a meal is being prepared. The routine – whatever it is – is unfamiliar. Your fear may be intensified by would-be adopters passing by and eyeballing you. Staring visitors are known to stress the wild cat species kept in zoos.[24]

How you cope with all this will depend on your temperament and the extent to which this new environment is cat friendly. If you are like most stray cats in well-run shelters, your stress levels should start to drop in the first four days. A hiding place within the pen, even if it is just a cardboard box, is the single most important feature that can help you cope. A fixed daily routine, with the same human carers, a relatively quiet environment, cleaning only half the pen at a time so that the other half retains your own scent, and the possibility of gentle and predictable human affection if you ask for it – all these will help your fear diminish. Some shelters even give their cats reward-training sessions with a clicker, which most cats enjoy, and which can make cats more adoptable.[25] Chaotic routines, changing human carers, lack of privacy, being moved from pen to pen, barren caging, frightening noises or rigid cleaning that does not respect your need to keep a familiar scent profile in the pen – all these may mean your stress remains high for two weeks or longer. In the worst-case scenario, if you are a very nervous cat in a poorly run shelter, your stress will not have even started to level off after two weeks. When researchers measured stress in cats at a boarding cattery, they found a small proportion of cats remained highly stressed throughout their two-week stay.[26] A good shelter should recognize if you are one of these stress-prone cats and put you in a foster home where there is, at least, more space and more places to hide.

Your ability to cope in the traditional rescue shelter will also depend on the level of expertise among the carers. Some of the human behaviours that upset you will be done in good faith, either for the sake of hygiene or even with the idea of 'taming' you. Humans may not recognize your inner stress from your behaviour – your hunched-up tense posture, the fact that you do not eat much and then only at night, your aggression when they try to handle you, or your hypervigilance. Or maybe you are just one of those cats that pretends to sleep so the carers think that you are merely 'quiet'.[27] If the shelter keeps good records, carers may at least notice that your food intake is low or that your bowels are affected. But they may not realize that behaviour like vomiting, bowel problems, decreased eating and drinking, and other sickness behaviours may be a sign of stress.[28] Finally, if they do not notice any of this, your continued distress may result in a serious upper respiratory infection. Indeed, a persistent high level of upper respiratory infection can be a marker of poor practice within a rescue shelter.

The sooner you can get out of your holding pen and into a home, the better it will be for you and the cheaper for the shelter. But here comes another potential problem. Is the shelter organized for a quick turnaround and your adoption? Do they put a good photograph online? Do they find you a 'good enough' home quickly, or do they wait months for what they see as your ideal owner? Are you even suitable as a pet cat in a normal home? And is their judgement of what will make a good owner based on your requirements or their requirements? Do they make sure that you have been neutered before you are handed over?

Matching cats to new homes can mean difficult conversations with eager would-be adopters. If you are badly matched to your new owner, you may find yourself in the wrong home or handed back and labelled as a cat with poor temperament. Or maybe you are abandoned for the second time in your life, discarded because the new unsatisfied owners want to avoid an embarrassing conversation with the rescue shelter. Or you simply go missing, because they did not keep you indoors long enough to let you familiarize yourself with your new home. These are the hazards that face you and other cats after being rescued.

EUTHANASIA – MENACE OR MERCY?

There are worse dangers, too. In some parts of the world, if you are 'rescued', you may not survive more than 24 hours. In the past, huge numbers of unwanted cats have simply been killed rather than rehomed. A survey of American animal shelters in 1997 reported that 71 per cent of the cats taken in were killed rather than adopted out, not just because they were unadoptable but due to overcrowding within the shelter.[29] Even in this century some animal-rescue organizations have been as much about euthanasia as rescue. Between 2006 and 2008 the RSPCA in Australia reported that 65 per cent of cats entering its Queensland rescue programme were euthanized rather than adopted.[30] The number dropped a few years later to only 15 per cent thanks to increased fostering and an innovative partnership with a retail pet chain.[31] In the United Kingdom, where no-kill animal shelters are common, in 2010 only about 13 per cent of the cats had to be put down and 77.1 per cent of the cats found a new owner, even though these shelters reported that they were usually or always full and many had waiting lists.[32]

If you are an elderly or a sick stray cat, your prospects are much worse. Most cat-rescue organizations will have to make a decision about your quality of life. Is it so poor that euthanasia is the best option for your welfare? Some cat lovers feel that if you are not diseased or in obvious pain you should nevertheless be given the chance for adoption, even if that involves a long time confined or even the rest of your life in a pen waiting for an adopter who never comes. Others argue that the quality of a life lived in a small pen is so poor that euthanasia would be the kinder option. Extended veterinary treatment in old age is a cost to the rescue and an emotional cost to you in terms of stressful vet visits during ill health. Your continued residence during veterinary treatment may mean that younger cats that should be admitted are turned away. Pen blocking can also occur because cat rescuers do not wish to face a decision to euthanize you even when it may be in your best interests to do so. There are no easy answers.

One major problem is that humans are not good at recognizing when you are in physical pain, let alone emotional pain. As a small animal, evolution has made you vulnerable to bigger carnivores, and obvious signs of pain would focus a predator's attention on you. Therefore, you do not usually whimper, whine or cry from pain unless it is extreme or sudden, although you may occasionally shriek from terror. Otherwise, you normally endure pain with silent stoicism. You show your pain only by increased inactivity, longer time spent sleeping, or dislike of petting, rather than by obvious limping or stiffness. The observant might spot a change in your face, a tighter muzzle and your ears separated more, and now computer technology will soon be able to help detect these.[33] A free app, the *Feline Grimace Scale*, helps cat professionals and experienced cat rescuers to recognize the facial signs of pain.[34] However, ordinary cat lovers without the app may fail to notice even quite obvious signs such as the 'plantigrade posture', where diseased cats walk on the back of the heel and the hock of their foot rather than on their toes. Carers may misinterpret your symptoms as 'old age' rather than as signs of pain or illness.

Your rescuers may also differ in whether they think your quality of life is good enough. Some will keep you in a pen too long; others may euthanize you too quickly. There is no single definition of quality of life, the factor that is crucial for a euthanasia decision. Most of the early definitions of animal welfare focused on the absence of the bad things in life – pain, suffering and discomfort, lack of food, water, shelter and veterinary care, and lack of social company where appropriate. Today there is a growing agreement that your quality of life should include not just an absence of bad things but the presence of good things – choice, control of your environment, play, interesting activities, and loving human contact if desired. The aim is to tot up the good and the bad, and make sure the good always predominates for either a good life or a life worth living. But your confinement in a rescue pen rarely includes positive experiences like choice, play or interesting activities.

Rescuers cannot ask you if your life is worth living, but they could focus on making sure you have positive experiences while in their care, not just good food and vet care. If you are lucky, they will keep your stay as short as possible, consider foster care if you are highly stressed, find the right kind of home for a cat like you, and be brave enough to make a euthanasia decision if your life is not worth living.

The truth is you were not rescued when you were picked up off the street. You were not rescued when you were in the rescue pen. You have only been rescued when you settle down into the kind of home where you can enjoy life.

11

WHAT IT IS LIKE BEING A PET

At last, you have a proper home with a loving human. The bond between a human and you can be as strong as the bond between humans and dogs and, if the details of dog-specific behaviour are omitted, both cats and dogs are an equal source of comfort to humans.[1] There are potential health benefits, too, for humans with a pet cat. Giving just one example, they may have a decreased risk of death due to heart problems.[2] In return for being a pet you get the benefit of regular meals, and you get a dry warm house even in the winter. In a cat-loving household you will also get taken to a vet for medical care if you are injured or ill. Being a pet cat will give you a longer life and a more comfortable one, but it can have its difficulties, too. Just like human relationships, the one between your human and you can be anything from a fairly remote relationship to a very close bond.[3] Sometimes, indeed, the relationship is the problem particularly if your human expects more affection than you are comfortable giving. Being a pampered pet is not always what you want or need if you are a very independent cat.

THE FIVE PILLARS OF FELINE BLISS

What do you need for a happy domestic life? The five pillars of a healthy feline environment, according to the American Association of Feline Practitioners and the International Society for Feline Medicine are:

1. A safe place.
2. Plenty of separated resources like food, water, toileting areas, scratching areas, play areas, and resting or sleeping areas.
3. The opportunity for play and predatory behaviour.
4. Positive, consistent and predictable human–cat social interactions.
5. An environment that respects the importance of the cat's sense of smell.[4]

A lifestyle with all these resources gives you choice and control over your life. There are also legal requirements for your welfare. In the UK, for example, under the Animal Welfare Act 2006, cat owners must make sure that you live in a suitable environment, eat a suitable diet, show normal behaviour patterns, are housed either with or without another animal (as appropriate), and are protected from pain, suffering, injury and disease. This reflects the fact that your quality of life will largely depend upon how your human cares for you. In Australia and the US it is more complicated. In Australia most of the responsibility for animal welfare is devolved to the individual states and territories, so legislation varies accordingly. In the US the federal welfare laws applying nationally exclude farm animals, and much of the welfare legislation for all animals varies from state to state.

In a cat-loving home, you can usually – though not always – find most of these five basic needs are catered for. But what a human owner thinks you need is not always what you feel you need – as a careful look at your home environment, your diet, how you behave, the other animals and humans in the house, and your encounters with veterinary care shows. Life in a pet home seen through feline eyes is not always as relaxed as it might seem to humans.

Your ability to live as a pet will also always partly depend on your individuality, your temperament and early life experiences. What is stressful for an animal or a human and how they cope with it vary in each individual.[5] Some cope by active attempts to change the stressful situation, while others passively endure it; many cats try both ways of coping. If you have a confident temperament and were educated in kittenhood for life in human households, you will cope better in a human home than if you are a cat with a nervous temperament which has not been brought up from kittenhood in a human home. Depending on your individual nature – and cats are very individual indeed – there may be aspects of being a pet that other cats find easy and enjoyable, but which make you anxious or fearful. This is bad for your emotional and physical health. If you are overwhelmed with stress or live with chronic stress, the stress-related chemicals in your body will start affecting not just your emotional health but also your physical health. Chronic stress reduces your lifespan, weakens your immune system, and makes you more vulnerable to diseases such as feline cystitis.[6] Moreover, owners may not recognize that you are showing signs of stress.[7]

SECURITY AND PREDICTABILITY

What kind of environment, the first requirement of the UK welfare laws, will make you happy and contented as a pet? A suitable environment is not just about how you are physically housed, it is also about safety and predictability. It is one that smells right, a home where you feel secure with familiar and friendly companions whether human, other cats or other domestic animals. A good home not only has to be safe but has to *feel* safe to you. A feeling of security is vital for you. Because in the wild cats are prey for other bigger animals, you have evolved to always be alert for potential dangers and will only relax when you feel you are in a safe environment. You carefully check out and regularly patrol both your core home area in the house and your hunting territory range outdoors in the garden, roads, and fields or parks. This regular patrolling helps you notice any change in the environment which you may need to know about.

Unpredictable environments always make your stress levels rise, so any change in your surroundings is important information for you. Anything new in the environment is potentially trouble for you. Of course, some stress in your life, and in the life of humans too, is unavoidable and animals can live with stress if in other ways they have a life worth living. When a danger or a difficulty is predictable and you know about it, you can make sure you respond in the right way. For example, if you know that the black-and-white cat down the street at house number 36 is hostile, you can just avoid the places or times where you might run into him. If the household is particularly busy, you will often chill out in an area where you can feel relaxed and secure. Your safe haven or a hiding place may be in a spare room where you can get away from noisy children or dogs, a cardboard box in the bedroom, or a cosy cat bed high up on top of a cupboard.

Routine and thus predictability are part of a suitable environment and are requirements for your serenity and welfare. Unpredictability is stressful in any feline life. When researchers evaluated laboratory cats for stress they found that changes in routine such as irregular feeding and cleaning times, unpredictable handling and an absence of talking and petting by caretakers made cats 'chronically stressed'.[8] Similarly, an altered household routine may stress you out, too, if it means food is put down at a different time, building work or redecoration is being done within or just outside the house, or humans are unexpectedly absent or present at different times. New human partners, visitors, workers, new cats, new dogs and new babies – all these can upset you. Indeed, new household members, whether human or animal strangers, may seem potentially dangerous to you, until you have checked them out carefully over days or even weeks. Besides, many of these changes to your house also bring new smells into the household and disrupt the existing family scent profile, making home feel less secure.[9]

Scents, many unnoticed by humans, influence your feelings of security hugely. If a human in the house gets a new job and comes home smelling of the disinfectant and scents you associate with vet visits, this can distress you. Just a visit to the vet by a companion cat can disrupt a feline friendship or a mutual tolerance between cats. Even in an otherwise good home, if you are a sensitive cat, cleaning by an obsessively house-proud human, or a human addicted to household scent plug-ins, can make your life as a pet feel stressful.

You either will have to go round all the familiar places replacing the family scent that cleaning has wiped away or try to compete with that strong floral scent from the plug-in that is flooding the living room. Your core territory has to be what you feel is a suitable environment, not what your human thinks is suitable.

Finally, there is the important issue of toilet facilities. For your comfort you need enough loose soil, sand or cat litter so that you can dig a hole and then cover your eliminations. Most cats also like to turn round and look at their elimination, before covering it up. The soil or litter should be reasonably dry and not dampened with other cat's excretions. The toilet area should be in a location which seems safe to you. You feel vulnerable while toileting, so a feeling of safety is important. Cat flaps give you a choice of toilet areas outside (and choice is often reassuring for you), but you may be expected to go out in all weathers. This can be tough on you when you are old or perhaps feeling ill. You may also find that your preferred safe area, whether it is in the neighbour's flower garden or under a garden shed, requires a journey through an enemy's territory. For these reasons you always require a litter tray inside the house, even if you do not use it much. This litter tray should typically be one and a half times the length of your body from nose to base of tail, and there should be at least 5cm (2in) of litter inside it. As a rule of thumb, it is safest with indoor-only cats to have one litter tray per cat and an extra one for choice. Your human, however, may refuse to provide more than one litter box, even though there are two or more cats.

What are suitable toilet arrangements for you are not always considered suitable by your human. You will probably prefer a small-grained litter while your human may opt for cheaper, large-pelleted litter. This may feel like sharp cobbles to your sensitive paws. Your human may use deodorant litter, which you do not like. Small litter boxes, which take up less space in the house, are also sometimes preferred by humans. While you prefer a litter box cleaned once or twice daily, your owner may choose to clean it only two or three times weekly. The utility room or the conservatory may seem a suitable place for your litter box in your human's eyes, but these can be locations without privacy from your point of view, with noisy washing machinery in the utility room or see-through glass in the conservatory where outdoor cats can peer in. So, these locations do not feel safe to you.

A SUITABLE DIET

Giving you a suitable diet is the second UK legal welfare requirement. Modern complete cat foods from reputable pet-food manufacturers have carefully formulated ingredients, so that they are a suitable diet for most cats. That does not mean that the odd bit of supplementation or mixing up is a problem, and it might even be beneficial. But it must be cat food, not dog food, because you have some dietary requirements that are not found in dog food. Your gut is designed to be carnivorous, and you get several essential food requirements from meat, rather than being able to synthesize them in the body like other animals. You need arginine and taurine, both amino acids, and also arachidonic acid, a fatty acid. These are typically obtained from meat, so some of the necessary protein in your diet should come from animal, not vegetable, products. Because of a high risk of nutritional deficiencies, you should not be a vegetarian or a vegan, whatever your human may believe. You require correct levels of various vitamins, too, like vitamin A, vitamin D and some B vitamins in your diet.[10] Therefore, home-made diets, home-mixed raw-food diets, supplementary treat foods, or cheap foods from countries where there is little regulation, may not keep you in long-term good health – the more so if you cannot supplement your diet with mammals or birds on the side.

And here's another problem. It's not just what humans feed you, but also how they feed you that can cause you problems. The way it is often given to you just in a bowl is not natural for your species. If you were eating the natural way, an ideal diet would be something like five or six little meals daily. To catch enough, you would probably have to make at least ten to twelve different hunting pounces, because many of your attempts would fail.[11] As a pet, you do not have to hunt for your food, and you may be fed only once or twice a day, which might mean you overfill your stomach at these times and that might predispose you to a range of health issues. If you are fed ad lib, with your food always left out for you, you can take ten small portions daily, which is more natural, but the downside is that some cats cannot regulate their feeding and will eat too much. Even if you are given an automatic feeder, timed to open on small portions every few hours, you are still not eating in a natural way, because you do not have to hunt before eating each portion. Worse still for an animal that does not share food with others, you may be forced to eat from a food bowl which is too close to another cat. As noted earlier, for a human a row of cats feeding from bowls looks cute; to you it is often stressful.

You may also have a human who just gives you too much food. In the human mind food is a way to express affection – friends give dinner parties, lovers woo with a meal out, friends give boxes of chocolates, and children are given sweets. Too many cat treats or too much food from your human's plate are the equivalent of junk food for humans, and, like humans, you may end up obese. Humans laugh at fat cats with their saggy tummies, but it is a serious health issue for you. Obesity can result in diabetes, augment any arthritic pain in old age, and contribute to other diseases. Living as you do in a human home, your diet depends largely on the good sense of your human, and some humans seem unable to stop overfeeding you

Water is another essential requirement, but because of your desert heritage you may not always drink much and suffer from hydration stress. One reason may be that your human places the water bowl near the food bowl, just like a glass put next to a plate on the human table. Unlike humans, you do not normally drink with your meals and, given a choice, you often prefer to drink in a different room.[12] This may be one of several reasons why you often drink from puddles or outside water sources, rather than the bowl indoors. Another minor difficulty for you is that you cannot focus clearly on the bowl or water surface when you are drinking, and if the bowl is located against a wall (as it frequently is), you may not be able to choose the position for drinking that you would prefer. If you are fed only dry food, you will drink about a third more water. You should always have more than one water bowl and more than one water location, particularly if you have the beginnings of kidney disease or suffer from cystitis. Choice may encourage you to drink more, but many humans do not give you enough choice.

FREEDOM TO BE A CAT

A third requirement for your welfare is that you should be able to show normal feline behaviour. Hunting, scratching and climbing are some of the normal behaviour patterns you need to express, and this is where life as a pet may have major deficiencies. The more your essential physical requirements are met, the more you need to be provided with these activities to be psychologically healthy. So, enriching your life with enjoyable activities becomes an essential requirement for most cats living in a human home. Inside the human home you can, at least, climb on windowsills and scratch the furniture if no scratching post is available. But there is usually no hunting inside the human home (unless you bring a mouse back!). To allow you to go in and out of the house at will, you may have a cat flap, ideally a microchip-operated one, which gives you choice and control over this hunting need. You can come and go, patrol your hunting range, and sometimes hunt and kill wildlife. Hunting which includes patrolling and searching for prey, whether or not you catch anything, keeps you active and mentally engaged. You fulfil one of the oldest instincts of your being while doing this and you also experience the emotional joy of desire and expectancy. If you have the opportunity for this normal behaviour, you are less likely to experience the stress of boredom, the lack of the right kind of space, the probability of overweight, or the development of abnormal behaviours such as overgrooming. If you have a cat flap you can also escape for some of the time from stressful conditions such as too many resident cats, too many humans, or frightening humans.

The downside is that cat-flap freedom and mental well-being

come at the expense of your physical health and safety. Outdoor hazards include busy roads, a high population of neighbouring cats, or roaming dogs. Road accidents, dog attacks and sometimes fights with other cats, particularly in the first few years of your life when you are at your most active, may injure or kill you.[13] There are also parasites and diseases. If you have a cat flap, you are nearly three times as likely than an indoor-only cat to get infected with round worms, tape worms, other internal parasites or viruses.[14] These you may catch from the soil, from your prey or from other cats.

The other disadvantage of a cat flap, not from your point of view but from a human point of view, is the impact that you and other free-roaming cats have on wildlife. A high meat content in your food and regular play with your human can reduce, but does not normally put an end to, the number of animals you kill.[15] Indeed, you may be required to be an indoor-only cat. Some countries may have local, regional or state legal restrictions of varying strictness against free-roaming cats. There may be cat curfews confining you to indoors during designated times or even prohibitions against being let outside at all. These restrictions are in place to protect wildlife from free-roaming cats, but this indoor-only life, unless mitigated by fenced garden enclosures[16] or good indoor activities, reduces the joy in your life. Indoor-only life is, in effect, life in captivity, though most cats adapt to if they are accustomed to it from an early age. In the hunting behaviour sequence of detecting, stalking, catching, killing and then eating prey, only the final stage, that of eating, may be available for you. And it is possible you may overeat as a reaction to that unavailability or to boredom.[17]

You will enjoy regular play sessions with fishing-rod toys operated by your human, but many humans do not teach you how to play safely in kittenhood or give you enough of this kind of play later in life. Unfortunately, you may also have learned in kittenhood to play with human body parts, such as fingers. With your tiny kitten teeth, your play may seem harmless, but with adult teeth it may cause physical damage and infection. Without any natural outlet for your need to hunt, humans may be the only moving creatures in your environment, which arouses your hunting instinct. Focusing on human body parts, you bite down hard, just as you would if you were breaking the neck of a mouse. In this way you can do quite severe damage. The bacteria on your teeth may cause serious infection, and untreated cat bites have been known to put humans on an antibiotic drip in hospital.

Other reactions to boredom may damage your relationship with your owner. Your attempts to cope with life as a pet may result in natural reactions like urine marking, toileting outside the litter tray, scratching furniture, or fighting with other cats. These are 'problem behaviours' in human eyes and more common among indoor-only cats.[18] From your point of view, they are natural behaviours in a difficult situation from which you cannot escape. To your owner, they are bad behaviours which they might think deserve punishment, which is not something that usually works or helps your relationship. You are not being deliberately nasty! Incompatible resident cats, dogs that frighten you, and humans that stress you out without meaning to are difficulties that you have to face whether you are an indoor-only or a cat-flap cat, but they are likely to be more intense if you are the former.

COMPANIONSHIP AND CONFLICT

A fourth requirement for a happy life is that your need for companionship should be met. But there are no fixed rules that apply to all cats. Your need for companionship or lack of it is very individual. Sociability with other cats is on a spectrum ranging from the very sociable individual that enjoys the company of another cat through to natural loners that detest all other cats. In the wild, unowned cats often live in related female groups with males that visit. Even within a female group some cats are more friendly to each other than others: they choose their close companions just as humans choose their friends. Unless you dislike all other cats (and some cats do), you will be friendly with one or two cats, tolerate some and hate others.

In a modern home, if you live with other cats, they are usually unrelated and they have been chosen not by you but by your human. Your feelings may resemble those of a human who is flat-sharing with strangers whom they dislike. If you have been homed with a sibling, or a cat you have known since the early days of kittenhood, it is more likely that you can be friends. With other unrelated cats, you may manage by time-sharing areas of the house, spacing yourselves out, and sometimes living in a different part of the house altogether, if the environment allows this. You may even find a friend among them. Lack of crowding, slow introductions for new cats, sensible cat-caring routines, plenty of resources and good house space help you and most cats live without conflict in a multi-cat household.[19, 20] However, if you are truly incompatible with another cat, or space is limited, there will be tension that your human may not even notice.

Fights, hissing, spitting and yowling do get human attention, but your human may not notice offensive staring, subtle bullying around beds, food bowls, water bowls, litter boxes and cat flaps, or be aware that a co-resident cat is blocking you or even moving you away from these resources.

Even if you can escape through the cat flap, there are potential problems with the neighbouring cats outside. In the wild, numbers are controlled by the amount of food available, but when cats are fed by humans, there is no limit on numbers. There may be despotic cats in the neighbourhood that fight every other feline on their patch,[21] or cats that break into your home, your supposedly secure territory, and steal your cat food. Intrusions into your safe core territory are very stressful for you, and you may feel the need to mark it with urine spraying. This natural response to your social anxiety is a problem for your human and is often misinterpreted as an action of bad behaviour which needs punishing. This can only make your anxiety more severe.

Another common crisis occurs when a new cat is brought into your household and simply placed in your environment without careful introductions.[22] The new cat smells unfamiliar to you, and you may see it as an intruder in your core territory. You can usually adjust to living with this new cat eventually, but a good relationship is far from inevitable. About four out of ten owners report signs of conflict between household cats such as staring, chasing, stalking, running away, tail twitching, hissing and screaming. These signs diminish only slowly, if at all.[23] As you have limited ways of reconciling yourself to another cat, and instead you deal with conflict by putting space between you and others, you may find it difficult to downplay initial aggression into mutual liking.[24] Very occasionally, household conflict is severe, resulting in fur and blood on the carpet or with a victim hiding all day on top of the wardrobe, only coming out at night to eat and eliminate. Even if there is no outright fighting, any alteration in the number of resident cats temporarily disrupts the family scent profile, which may make for new tensions between the cats. Even absence, when one cat dies or is rehomed, may change the familiar family scent profile for the worse. Weeks and sometimes months of subtle aggressive behaviours, unnoticed by the owner, may result in tension among cats. A particularly difficult situation occurs if you are an elderly cat that has lost your companion. Well-meaning owners may add a kitten 'as a friend' and you find yourself being harassed by a playful youngster. All your difficulties with other resident cats result from the human lack of knowledge about feline sociability and the difficulty of choosing a new cat that is compatible with existing residents.

The other animal you are housed with is a human or several humans. You usually fit into human life reasonably well, although your stress levels may increase in a household that has too many humans for you and not enough space to avoid them. Owners that have a busy social life may stress you out due to visitors to or social gatherings within the house, particularly if you are a single cat.[25] You prefer familiar humans and a familiar routine. Ironically, you can also have problems with owners who love you too much. They may behave in ways that upset you without meaning to. Humans who lovingly gaze at you, for instance, may make you feel uneasy. You typically experience staring by other cats as hostile, so you may react to a direct human gaze by breaking off eye contact. If they are close, you may blink more frequently, another way of avoiding the human stare.[26]

CAT CUDDLES – RIGHTS AND WRONGS

Another human–cat misunderstanding is petting. Humans enjoy extended periods of affectionate cuddling and often like the close, restricting contact of a body hug. Your affectionate rubs against other cats are usually brief, and you may not enjoy extended petting or close-contact cuddling, unless you have been cuddled a lot as a kitten. Your feline reaction will vary from placid enjoyment, through tense toleration, to dislike and escape. By measuring the level of stress hormones in faeces, researchers found that cats that merely tolerated petting, rather than enjoying it, had higher stress levels than cats that enjoyed it. Those cats that disliked petting, on the other hand, did not have higher stress levels, perhaps because they successfully avoided being petted in the first place.[27] You may also put an end to unwanted petting with a nip, the so-called *petting and biting syndrome*, a common feline reaction.[28] It is difficult to know how else you could tell a human to stop, yet some ignorant humans will thereby label you as 'vicious' or 'nasty', when you are really just expressing yourself in a natural way.

Human hands intruding in body areas you consider private are also not welcome. If you are like most cats, you will prefer to be stroked round the head and cheek but may not enjoy being stroked at the base of the tail.[29] You may also dislike any human attempt to give you a tummy rub and may well respond by raking the intruding hand with your back claws. Like most cats you will probably not want your sensitive paw pads touched either. You like to control the affectionate interaction between you and a human. If you ask for and choose petting, it is more acceptable to you and the session will last longer. If the human is the one to start the petting, you will usually opt for a shorter session.[30] If you feel your human is harassing you for affection, you have only two options – either to walk away or to nip and scratch. The latter works well, because the human hand is normally withdrawn promptly, so you learn how to deal with any unwanted affection in the future. Punishment will make you even more wary of letting human hands near you and will make your stress worse.

These then are some of the problems that you can face in a human home. Most of them arise because humans do not understand your underlying nature. (There is more on the mysteries of cat behaviour in Appendix 2.) In the final short chapter, we will sum up what you typically want from your human.

12

WHAT YOU AS A CAT
WANT – CHOICE AND CONTROL

As a cat you want some control over your environment that will give you choices in your life – not just deciding, as you dither in the doorway when your human has opened the door for you, whether you go in or out! There are more important choices for you such as where and when you eat, where you feel safe enough to toilet, where you choose to drink, where you feel relaxed enough to have a long deep sleep, how close you sleep to your human, whether you want to be on a human lap, and whether you choose to be stroked or not. All these are choices that give you some control over your life, but many of them depend on your human's behaviour. So, it is important that your human gives you the freedom to make as many choices as possible. You want to be able to make your own decisions. It also means that your human should treat you like an individual because your preferences will be individual ones.

You know, and now human scientists know, that every cat has a different personality, with different likes and dislikes, and with an individual attitude towards humans and towards other cats. There are no one-size-fits-all rules for your happiness. Your lifestyle, which ranges from complete independence from humans to close loving bonds with them, should also be respected. If this principle of giving you choices in your life is adopted by all cat lovers, whether rescuers or those who have made a cat part of the family, you have a good chance of leading a happy life.

Your attitude to humans will vary. If you are an adult feral cat or a street cat, you should not be forced to live in a human home, to be 'tamed' or kept in a pen or small enclosure. If you are a kitten that is going to be a human pet, humans should give you the best start in life, by handling you gently and teaching you how to enjoy human touch in the first eight weeks of your life. The UK charity Cats Protection supplies a chart and video showing how to do this,[1] and it should be done by all breeders and rescuers. When you go to your new human home, you need neutering by four months at the latest, if you have not already had this done.[2] Too many kittens are born because humans have left neutering too late. Microchipping and vaccinations against common diseases should be done during this period, too. Even if you are going to be an indoor-only cat, vaccination is a good idea, since even indoor-only cats may sometimes escape into or get lost in the wider world. Yearly vaccination also gives you the chance for a free annual veterinary check-up.

As a pet cat, you need a human who will accept you as you are and not force you to be a cuddle cat if you do not like cuddles. If you are a cat that needs your own space, you will want that space respected. You will not enjoy being picked up and kissed, petted in private areas where you do not like being touched, or simply being persistently petted when you have had enough. Even cat lovers who have kept cats all their lives can sometimes fail to understand this and persist in unwanted affectionate touching.[3] Unwelcome behaviour like this violates your personal autonomy and makes you more wary of your human companion. Humans that do this are risking a good cat–human relationship. The true cat lover waits for you to initiate petting, learns what you like best and stops before you have had enough. Humans who wish to know if you want to be stroked should present a fist to see if you rub against it in what might be called the *cat consent test*.[4] That way you are more likely to enjoy being close to them. You may not want to jump on a human lap, but you may like being curled up next to them on the sofa. If your desire for closeness is respected, you may perhaps grow to want more human affection as you become older. You may also enjoy human attention more if it is done as playing rather than petting.

It would help if your human (or human rescuers) learned a little bit more about cat body language and cat behaviour. Reading books is not for everybody, but there are now good videos online which will help. That means keeping up to date with research, rather than relying on traditional folk wisdom. For example, historically it was advised that people put their cats out at night; up-to-date cat lovers usually close the cat flap at night because they know their cats will be at risk of traffic accidents or predators in the dark. Besides, in winter it is cold and wet.

There are some resources in a human home which are needed by almost all household cats. You may prefer to go out of the cat flap and eliminate in the garden, but a large litter tray with plenty of litter should also be provided indoors anyway. This gives you choice if the weather is horrible or when you get old and want to stay inside more. If you are an indoor-only cat, a second litter tray, in a second location, will give you the choice of using either – useful if you suddenly decide, as some cats do, that you need one tray for urine and a different one for faeces, or if you take a dislike to one of the trays. This choice may be incomprehensible to your human, but you make it nonetheless! A wise human also always respects your preferred choice of litter and, if the litter type must be changed, does this slowly, handful by handful, over several weeks. If you do suddenly start house soiling, your human should get veterinary help to check for disease and then help from a behaviour expert if illness is not the cause (see Appendix 1).

Most cats in Europe are kept in homes where they have access to the great outdoors through a cat flap. In Australia, New Zealand and the US, the proportion of cat-flap cats is falling due to veterinary and conservation disapproval. However, whatever the conservation issues, a cat flap gives you the chance to patrol your area, laze in a sunny garden, walk on the walls and fences that are preferred feline roadways and, if you are lucky, do a bit of hunting. Cat flaps with microchips allow you to retreat into the home without the fear of other cats intruding. This enjoyable lifestyle gives you plenty of activity, even if there is the risk of traffic accidents or predators. If you have become used to the cat-flap lifestyle, you should not be forced into the life of an indoor-only cat, except for a very good reason such as disability, infectious disease or old age. Kittens that have never known the outside life are the best choice for indoor-only cats.

If you are an indoor-only cat, you need more activity. Boredom is stressful for you. Cat trees, high shelving walkways, and hiding places can make a room into a cat palace. Cat toys, food dispensers and even cat wheels for some cats help keep you active. Best of all is a human who gives you regular play sessions with an appropriate cat toy. What you will enjoy most is a toy that is a moving target, not just a static one. Toys should be changed regularly. Playing with another cat is also valuable social enjoyment if, and only if, you are lucky enough to have a bonded companion cat (your sibling, for instance). Not every cat will make a compatible companion, and if you fall out with your indoor companion cat, your human may need expert advice to help you live together in mutual toleration, if not friendship. Some helpful websites and organizations can be found in Appendix 1.

Your attitude to other cats should also be respected by your human. You may be a loner that wants to be the only cat in the household and dislikes all other cats, or you may be a more sociable individual that can get on with some, though not all, cats. What you usually do not want is the sudden arrival of a strange adult cat that you did not choose. It is unlikely you will be instantly friendly with a feline stranger, which does not have the family smell, dumped in your territory. But you may eventually accept the newcomer if your human arranges a careful introduction over a number of weeks.[5] The same care is needed if a new dog is added to the family.[6] If you have never lived with a dog before, a new puppy arriving suddenly may feel like a dangerous beast, and your humans should take the greatest care not to alarm you and to keep you safe. If you have lived with a family dog before, you will not find this as difficult, but you still need a careful and safe introduction. Humans who just add a dog to a cat household without an introduction plan are putting your security and happiness at risk.

Finally, if your human fills the house with too many cats, they are not doing you a favour. To get on with other cats, you and the others need to practise mutual avoidance and social distancing. This means you must be able to choose to sleep at a suitable distance, eat at a distance and eliminate privately. This requires plenty of resources (beds, dishes and litter trays) and enough space, including high spaces, to keep away from each other. One rule of thumb is that a household with two bedrooms has space for two cats or three at the maximum.

If problems arise and you behave in a way that upsets your human, you should never be punished. The study of animal behaviour has shown that human punishment of an animal, whether a dog or a cat, is rarely effective as it is often totally misunderstood by the animal. Moreover, it can ruin the human–cat relationship. If you are house soiling or scratching the wrong areas, you will often do this more frequently if you are punished. If you have a cat flap, you may leave home if you feel unsafe in the household. So, a human who decided to train a cat should use reward-based training, also known as *positive reinforcement*. There are books and videos online for this, too.

So, what is the ideal human for you? They should love cats, of course, but love is not enough. They should be ready to learn more about cats. They should adopt rather than buy a cat whenever possible, understanding that most good pedigree cat clubs have a rescue section for those who want a pedigree. They should also have enough money to keep a cat and should consider cat insurance for unexpected veterinary bills. People on low incomes should investigate any nearby charities that offer free veterinary care, before getting a cat. If free veterinary care is not available to them, they might benefit from becoming a fosterer for a rescue shelter, which will pay the bills for their foster cat.

Most of all, your human should respect you as a unique furry personality and give you choice and control in your life.

APPENDIX 1: USEFUL ORGANIZATIONS, WEBSITES AND OTHER RESOURCES

ASPCA. www.aspca.org
Runs local shelters, promotes neutering, gives basic cat-care advice and helps stop cruelty to cats and other animals in the US.

Association of Pet Behaviour Counsellors. https://www.apbc.org.uk/
These are qualified behaviour counsellors working with animals that have been referred by a vet. All good behaviour counsellors require a veterinary referral.

The Australian Pet Welfare Foundation. https://petwelfare.org.au/
A research and advocacy body that is running Trap Neuter and Return cat programmes.

Cat handling from Battersea Dogs and Cats Home.
https://www.youtube.com/watch?v=UwqG2wLb0KQ
A really clear video.

Cats Protection. www.cats.org.uk
This is the UK's biggest cat-rescue charity and you can easily find a cat for adoption on its website. It also has good cat advice.

Celia Haddon's cat website. www.catexpert.co.uk
This has advice on common cat problems like house soiling, litter-tray dislike, cat fighting, indoor-only cat ideas, and cats that bite humans.

Daniel Mills YouTube podcast series 'What makes you click?'
https://www.facebook.com/dsmpod
This features chats with inspirational friends in the field of
animal behaviour.

The Humane Society of the United States.
https://www.humanesociety.org
Useful information about helping community cats.

Indoor Cat website from Ohio State University.
https://indoorpet.osu.edu/cats
This has good ideas on how to keep an indoor-only cat happy.
For more ideas, see www.catexpert.co.uk

International Cat Care. www.icatcare.org
An international website that has everything you need to know
about rescuing cats, cat diseases, cat obesity and cat behaviour.
Icatcare's courses are also excellent and include a really good online
course for cat rescuers.

Meowsic website. www.meowsic.se
Susanne Schötz's website has everything you would like to know
about cat vocal noises.

Orphaned kittens that are found outdoors – a webinar.
https://www.facebook.com/kittenxlady/videos/236478304345838

RSPCA Australia. www.rspca.org.au
A good place to start for cat knowledge of any kind, including cat
welfare and cat behavioural needs.

APPENDIX 2: THE MYSTERIES OF CAT BEHAVIOUR

Many of the mysteries of your cat behaviour become clearer if humans put themselves into your place. In your world what makes good sense to you may seem bizarre to a human. Add to this the individuality of cat behaviour and it is no wonder that sometimes your actions seem odd to your humans. Here are some of the common moments when your cat behaviour mystifies many human onlookers and why they make perfect sense to you in your world.

Why do you go up to the only person in the room who doesn't like cats?

Visitors who dislike cats will usually keep their distance from you. They will not gaze at you, try to get close to you or try to pet you. So why do you want to go up to them and seem to ask for petting? In your view, there is a very good reason for this. From your perspective, a human who either avoids or ignores you is giving you the choice whether to get close or not. If you are a nervous cat, you will feel more in control and so you may well decide this person is worth knowing better. Indeed, when you can choose and control the petting, the petting session is likely to go on longer than if the session is chosen by the human.[1]

There is also the stare factor! In cat encounters, staring is rude and possibly even intimidating. So, you may be wary of people who stare at you, and visitors who love cats will often want to gaze lovingly at the household pet. Cat haters or those who feel unsure around cats, on the other hand, do not make eye contact. It is reassuring for you to meet a human who is behaving with good feline manners by not staring.[2] If you are a cat that is confident around humans, you may also want to mark the new person in your environment. By going over and rubbing against their body, you can sample the person's smell, add your own, update the household scent mix and potentially deposit chemicals which reassure you about this new feature in your home. Just like that shopping bag from the local supermarket!

Why do you prefer drinking from a running tap or toilet bowl rather than from your own water bowl?

Cats are very individual in their drinking habits, so you may well be one of these cats that enjoy a running tap or even the water in a toilet bowl.[3] One reason for this preference may be that the water from the tap or the toilet bowl is cooler than the water in your bowl. It may also be fresher. Not all humans change the water in your bowl daily, and you may well dislike dust on the water surface. Moreover, you may be a cat that combines drinking from the tap with playing with the water.[4] As it comes out, the water catches the light and makes an interesting moving, if liquid, target. You may also be intrigued by the flushing mechanism of the toilet. Scientists have tried to find out whether, as a general rule, cats preferred a water bowl or a pet fountain with flowing water, but they could only conclude that it just was a matter of individual choice.[5]

Another possibility is that the location of your water bowl does not suit you. Water is often in a bowl next to the food bowl and, as we have explained, you prefer to drink and eat at different locations.[6] As a small animal, you also need to feel secure while drinking, so a bowl that is put next to a wall means you must face the wall to drink. You may feel uneasy about not being able to check up what is happening in the room behind you.

If you have outdoor access, you may prefer drinking from ponds and puddles for the same reason. Also, as you can taste water, it is possible that these outside water sources taste better to you than the chemically treated tap water in human homes. That doesn't necessarily mean you want bottled water at home, though. When cats in a shelter were given either purified water or tap water, they drank more tap water than purified water![7] So if you ever have to go to the vets or cattery for an overnight stay, it is worth your owner taking some water from home for you, as you prefer the familiar. This will help to minimize the risks of dehydration.

Videos on the internet show that you and other cats are frightened of cucumbers. Why on earth should a cucumber terrify you?

You may jump away in fear when a cucumber is put behind you while you are eating and cannot see it. Your human may think it funny. You would not be frightened of a cucumber if it was just left lying about the house and indeed you might even enjoy eating a little bit of it. Some cats do. What makes you frightened is the fact that you cannot see it being placed there and it seems so strange.

Your frightened reaction makes sense. As a small animal, you have evolved to make sure you are safe from enemies, and you have an excellent automatic startle reflex to protect you from any unexpected danger. This same reflex reaction is seen in humans when a sudden noise makes them jump. Your brain activates this startle reflex in less than a second to ensure you are better safe than sorry in any potentially dangerous circumstance, and that means any circumstance when there is a big mismatch between what you expect to see in the world and what you actually see.[8]

As you turn away from your bowl, an unexpected object, the cucumber, suddenly comes into view and your startle reflex kicks in immediately. You automatically jump away to stay safe, even before you have time to fully assess what the object might be. Some humans may find this scenario funny, but for you this situation, particularly if it occurs more than once, may add to your general stress levels. You may even begin to feel nervous around the humans who tease you in this way or around the food bowl. This particular human craze, alas, is just one of many online video trends where cats are teased or even ill-treated for human amusement. Who knows what the next fad will be?

Why do you bring gifts in for your humans?

Your habit of bringing prey, dead or alive, into the house is one that both mystifies and upsets your humans. Are you bringing in a food present for the human you love? Or do you think your human is a large hairless kitten who needs to be taught how to catch mice? No. The explanation is simpler. It is about small-animal food security. Apart from bringing in prey for your kittens, you do not share food or give food as presents. The reason you bring prey into the house is that this is a safe place where you may bring new resources to potentially play with or consume later on. It is actually a sign of confidence. You bring prey to your safe place, without the fear that some large animal will pounce on you, where you can relax and do what you want with your prey, which might include just ignoring it! Your tendency to do this is also related to your personality, with it being more common among cat extraverts and those cats who score low for neuroticism (anxiety). So it is a sign of your confident personality when you bring home prey.[9]

So, what can your human do to persuade you not to bring back prey into the house? What might reduce the number of corpses brought in? While there are various contraptions on the market, it has been found that feeding you a high-meat diet and giving you five to ten minutes of play every day with a moving object may reduce, if not entirely stop, the numbers of birds and mammals being brought home, according to one study.[10] Cat bells on the collar had no effect in this study (though they have had some effect in other studies), but a Birdsbesafe ruff-like collar reduced the number of birds brought home.

Why do you do mad rushes, or zoomies, around the house?

Sudden bursts of running round the house or garden can be part of play. It is just fun to run and experience the world at high speed. It keeps your co-ordination skills fine-tuned. If your human pays attention to you when you do this, or even joins in the game by chasing you, that's even more fun. You may be one of those ingenious cats that have discovered you can get human attention and laughter by running up trees, doing a wall of death circle in an empty bath, or a zoomie circuit of the stairs. If you are an indoor-only cat, zoomies are also a fun way to use up extra energy after sleeping on the bed all morning. There is even a scientific term for zoomies which is *frantic random activity periods.*

You may be a cat that zooms at a regular time of day. This could be after eating a meal, when your blood sugar spikes and puts you in the mood for play. Or it may be at a regular time during the normal household routine, perhaps when your human comes home from work or has just finished their dinner, a time when they will notice this activity and pay extra attention to you. If you are a cat that zooms at 3am, it may be that your human should give you more to do during the day with regular fishing-rod play sessions.

Alternatively, you may be a cat that zooms after you have used the litter tray. This could be a response to a dirty tray, the need to get out of it as soon as possible leading to this bit of fun. If so, your human should clean the tray more often, at least twice a day or whenever they see it has been used. Or are you zooming out of the tray in relief from having done a difficult elimination? Your human should inspect to see if you are suffering from constipation.

Finally, if you are a cat that is not given to doing zoomies, yet you suddenly start to behave in a randomly overactive manner, this could be a sign that something is wrong. General overactivity and out-of-character restlessness, particularly in older cats, need a vet's attention.

Why do you suddenly start watching the TV when golf or football comes on?

Your vision is designed to attend to moving targets. You use simple cues to detect certain prey. Static images are of little interest to you.

Even if you see a flickering rather than a continuous image on the screen, this moving image may well get your attention.[11] A black-and-white moving football stands out well on the screen. A close-up of a white golf ball rolling towards, then disappearing into, a hole is also likely to stand out from the background and get noticed for its movement. Your attention is like a spotlight and is focused on a detail like a ball, rather than on the screen as a whole.

A straw poll in a newspaper some years ago showed that, among cats that took an interest in TV, the programmes they favoured were those with wildlife, so you also like wildlife detail, too. With your excellent hearing range, you may well detect and also be interested by ultrasonic sounds emitted from the TV, sounds that your human cannot hear.[12] Moving rodent shapes and bird shapes will also be of interest. There is also a third factor at work. You may discover that your human laughs or pays extra attention to you when you show interest in a TV programme. If you enjoy human attention, as many cats do, this will encourage you to demonstrate that you are interested.

Why are you so fascinated by boxes?

Boxes offer you a place of security, warmth and the opportunity for play. Security is perhaps the most important advantage because a box is a barrier between you and the potentially scary world around you. If you are a cat in a shelter, you will be less stressed if you have an enclosed space to hide in, even if it is just a cardboard box.[13] Even the low rim of a litter tray will give you a feeling of some protection against the world, in the same way your human might have a blanket that they like to wrap themselves in and snuggle down with to relax. Pedigree cats at a cat show or cats in a bare veterinary cage often retreat to their litter tray.

Boxes also offer you a nice place to sleep because your body warmth stays inside the box and you are protected from draughts. If you are a kitten or a playful adult cat, jumping in and out of a box may be part of playful exercise. However, your attraction to boxes goes further. If the outline of a square box is marked on the floor, you are likely to go and sit in it, as if it were a 3D box rather than just a 2D one! Some ingenious researchers did a citizen science experiment in which they asked cat owners to place what is called 'the Kanizsa square illusion' pattern, a similar but non-square Kanizsa pattern and a simple square pattern on the floor. Owners reported that their cats showed a preference for the Kanizsa square and the simple square, rather than the non-square pattern. 'If I fits I sits . . .' was the title of the study.[14]

ENDNOTES

INTRODUCTION: WHAT IS IT LIKE TO BE YOUR CAT?

1. Uexküll, J von (1992). A stroll through the worlds of animals and men: A picture book of invisible worlds. *Semiotica* 89, 319–91.
2. Ibid.
3. Ibid.
4. Nagel, T (1974). What is it like to be a bat? *The Philosophical Review* 83, 439–50.
5. Ibid.
6. Morgan, C L (1903). *An Introduction to Comparative Psychology*, 2nd edition. London: W. Scott, 59.
7. Skinner, B F (1953). *Science and Human Behavior*. New York: Macmillan, 160.
8. Malebranche, N (1689) as cited in Henriques, G (2022). *Are Animals Conscious?* Available at www.psychologytoday.com/gb/blog/theory-knowledge/202012/are-animals-conscious (last accessed 25 October 2022).
9. Low, P, Panksepp, J, Reiss, D, Edelman, D and Van Swinderen, B (2012). The Cambridge Declaration on Consciousness. Presented at the Francis Crick Memorial Conference on Consciousness in Human and Non-Human Animals, Churchill College, University of Cambridge, Cambridge, UK, 7 July 2012.
10. Butterfield, M E, Hill, S E and Lord, C G (2012). Mangy mutt or furry friend? Anthropomorphism promotes animal welfare. *Journal of Experimental Social Psychology* 48, 957–60.

CHAPTER ONE:
WHAT IT IS LIKE BEING IN YOUR FELINE BODY

1. Darwin, C (1859). *On the Origin of Species by Means of Natural Selection, or the Preservation of Favoured Races in the Struggle for Life*. London: John Murray.
2. Gough-Palmer, A L, Maclachlan, J and Routh, A (2008). Paws for thought: comparative radio-logic anatomy of the mammalian forelimb. *Radiographics*: 28, 501–10.
3. Bishop, K L, Pai, A K and Schmitt, D (2008). Whole body mechanics of stealthy walking in cats. *PLoS One* 3, e3808.
4. Fear Free Happy Homes (2022). What movement and gait tell you about your cat. Available at https://www.fearfreehappyhomes.com/what-movement-and-gait-tell-you-about-your-cat (last accessed 10 May 2022).
5. Bhatti, Z, Waqas, A, Mahesar, W and Karbasi, M (2017). Gait analysis and biomechanics of quadruped motion for procedural animation and robotic

simulation. *Bharia University Journal of Information and Communication Technologi (BUJICT)* 10, 1–7.

6. Walker, C, Vierck, C J and Ritz, L A (1998). Balance in the cat: role of the tail and effects of sacrocaudal transection. *Behavioural Brain Research* 91, 41–47.

7. Jusufi, A, Zeng, Y, Full, R J and Dudley, R (2011). Aerial righting reflexes in flightless animals. *Integrative and Comparative Biology* 51, 937–43.

8. Noel, A C and Hu, D L (2018). Cats use hollow papillae to wick saliva into fur. *PNAS* 115, 12377–82.

CHAPTER TWO:
HOW YOUR ANCESTORS BECAME PETS

1. Filhol, H (1891). *Étude des mammifères fossiles de Saint-Gérand-le-Puy (Allier)*. Available at https://babel.hathitrust.org/cgi/pt?id=ucbk.ark:/28722/h2r785q8r& view=1up&seq=200&q1=proailurus (last accessed 8 August 2021) [translated by the author].

2. Wikipedia (2022). Taxonomic rank. Available at https://en.wikipedia.org/wiki/ Taxonomic_rank (last accessed 17 May 2022). This provides a useful explanation of how biologists categorize and rank animals in groups.

3. Werdelin, L, Yamaguchi, N, Johnson, W E and O'Brien, S J (2010). Phylogeny and evolution of cats (Felidae). *Biology and Conservation of Wild Felids*, ed. D W Macdonald and A J Loveridge. Oxford: Oxford University Press, 59–82.

4. Loyd, K A T, Hernandez, S M, Carroll, J P, Abernathy, K J and Marshall, G J (2013). Quantifying free-roaming domestic cat predation using animal-borne video cameras. *Biological Conservation* 160, 183–9.

5. Cats Protection (2021). Pregnant cats, birth and care of young kittens. Available at https://www.cats.org.uk>media>eg18_pregnant_cats-birth_and_care_of_young_ kittens.pdf (last accessed 26 November 2021).

6. Silwa, A, Herbst, M and Mills, M G L (2010). Black-footed cats (*Felis nigripes*) and African wildcats (*Felis silvestris*): a comparison of two small felids from South African arid lands, in *Biology and Conservation of Wild Felids*, ed. D W Macdonald and A J Loveridge. Oxford: Oxford University Press, 537–58.

7. Driscoll, C A, Clutton-Brock, J, Kitchener, A C and O'Brien, S J (2009). The taming of the cat. *Scientific American* 300, 68–75.

8. Vigne, J-D, Guilaine, J, Debue, K, Haye, L and Gerard, P (2004). Early taming of the cat in Cyprus. *Science* 304, 259.

9. Vigne, J-D and Guilaine, J. (2004). 'Les premiers animaux de compagnie, 8500 ans avant notre ère? . . . ou comment j'ai mangé mon chat, mon chien et mon renard. *Anthropozoologica* 39, 249–73.

10. Malek, J (1993). *The Cat in Ancient Egypt*. London: The British Museum Press.

11. Ibid.

12. Herodotus (2022). *Histories* 2, 66–67, translated by Godley, A D. Available at www.perseus.tufts.edu/hopper/text?doc=Perseus%3Atext%3A1999.01.0126%3A book%3D2%3Achapter%3D66 (last accessed 31 October, 2022).

13. Driscoll et al. (2009).

14. Finka, L (2022). Conspecific and human sociality in the domestic cat: consideration of proximate mechanisms, human selection and implications for cat welfare. *Animals* 12, 298.

CHAPTER THREE:
WHAT IT IS LIKE BEING A KITTEN

1. Say, L, Pontier, D and Natoli, E (1999). High variation in multiple paternity of domestic cats (*Felis catus L.*) in relation to environmental conditions. *Proceedings of the Royal Society London* 266, 2071–4.

2. Reisner, L R, Houpt, K A, Erb, H N and Quimby, F W (1994). Friendliness to humans and defensive aggression in cats: the influence of handling and paternity. *Physiology and Behavior* 55, 1119–24.

3. Marchei, P, Diverio, S, Falocci, N, Fatjo, J, Ruiz-de-la-Torre, J L and Manteca, X (2011). Breed differences in behavioural response to challenging situations in kittens. *Physiology and Behavior* 102, 276–84.

4. Menotti-Raymond, M, David, V A, Pflueger, S M, Lindblad-Toh, K, Wade, C M, O'Brien, S J and Johnson, W E (2008). Patterns of molecular genetic variation among cat breeds. *Genomics* 91, 1–11.

5. Raihani, G, Rodriguez, A, Saldaña, A, Guarneros, M and Husdon, R (2014). A proposal for assessing individual differences in behaviour during early development in the domestic cat. *Applied Animal Behaviour Science* 154, 48–56.

6. Bateman, P. (2000). Behavioural development in the cat. In *The Domestic Cat: The Biology of Its Behaviour*, ed. D C Turner and P Bateson, 2nd edn. Cambridge: Cambridge University Press, 23–46.

7. Bateson, P, Mendl, M and Feaver, J (1990). Play in the domestic cat is enhanced by rationing of the mother during lactation. *Animal Behaviour* 40, 514–25.

8. Weinstock, M (2008). The long-term behavioural consequences of prenatal stress. *Neuroscience and Biobehavioural Reviews* 32, 1073–86.

9. Hepper, P G, Wells, D L, Millsopp, S, Kraehenbuehl, K, Lyn, S A and Mauroux, O (2012). Prenatal and early sucking influences on dietary preference in newborn, weaning, and young adult cats. *Chemical Senses* 37, 755–66.

10. Meaney, M J (2001). Maternal care, gene expression, and the transmission of individual differences in stress reactivity across generations. *Annual Review of Neuroscience* 24, 1161–92.

11. Little, S (2013). Playing mum: successful management of orphaned kittens. *Journal of Feline Medicine and Surgery* 15, 201–10.

12. Mills, D, Crisp, A, Ellis, S, Le Brech, S L and Bessant, C (no date). Hand rearing kittens: what do we know? Unpublished PowerPoint.

13. Ibid.

14. Ahola, M K, Vapalahti, K and Lohi, H (2017). Early weaning increases aggression and stereotypic behaviour in cats. *Nature Scientific Reports* 7, 1–9.

15. Bateson, P (2000). Behavioural development in the cat. In *The Domestic Cat: The Biology of Its Behaviour*, ed. D C Turner and P Bateson, 2nd edn. Cambridge: Cambridge University Press, 9–22.

16. Mermet, N, Coureaud, G, McGrane, S and Schaal, B (2008). Odour-guided social behaviour in newborn and young cats: an analytical survey. *Chemoecology* 17, 187–99.

17. Szenczi, P, Urrutia, A, Hudson, R and Banszegim, O (2021). Are you my mummy? Long-term olfactory memory of mother's body odour by offspring in the domestic cat. *Animal Cognition* 25, 21–6.

18. Beaver, B V (2003). *Feline Behavior: A Guide for Veterinarians*, 2nd edn. St Louis, MO: Saunders.

19. Ibid.

20. Ibid.

21. Bateson (2000).

22. Ibid.

23. Beaver (2003).

24. Casey, R A and Bradshaw, J W S (2008). The effects of additional socialisation for kittens in a rescue centre on their behaviour and suitability as a pet. *Applied Animal Behaviour Science* 114, 196–205.

25. Ibid.

26. Finka, L R (2022). Conspecific and human sociality in the domestic cat: consideration of proximate mechanisms, human selection and implications for cat welfare. *Animals* 12, 298.

27. Casey and Bradshaw (2008).

28. Finka (2022).

29. Turner, D (2000). The human–cat relationship. *The Domestic Cat: The Biology of Its Behaviour*, ed. D C Turner and P Bateson, 2nd edn. Cambridge: Cambridge University Press, 193–206.

30. Ibid.

31. Mendoza, D L and Ramirez, J M (1987). Play in kittens (*Felis domesticus*) and its association with cohesion and aggression. *Bulletin of the Psychonomic Society* 25, 27–30.

32. Joyce, A and Yates, D (2011). Help stop teenage pregnancy! Early-age neutering in cats. *Journal of Feline Medicine and Surgery*, 13, 3-10.

33. Beaver (2003).

34. Pachel, C L (2014). Intercat aggression: restoring harmony in the home: a guide for practitioners. *Veterinary Clinics of North America: Small Animal Practice* 44, 565–79.

CHAPTER FOUR:
WHAT YOU SEE AND HEAR AS A CAT

1. Miller, P E (2001). Vision in animals – what do dogs and cats see? *The 25th Annual Waltham/OSU Symposium. Small Animal Opthalmology*, 27–8. Available at: https://www.vin.com/apputil/content/defaultadv1.aspx?pId=11132&id=3844144 (last accessed 2 April 2021).

2. Ofri, R. (2008). Vision in the animal kingdom. *Proceedings of the 33rd World Small Animal Veterinary Congress*, 242–4.

3. Miller (2001).

4. Ofri, R (2020). Do dogs really see in black and white? Facts and myths about animal vision. *The Webinar Vet.* Available at www.thewebinarvet.com/webinar/do-dogs-really-see-in-black-white-facts-and-myths-about-animal-vision (last accessed 2 April 2021).

5. Miller (2001).

6. Ibid.

7. Ibid.

8. Ibid.

9. Clark, D L and Clark, R A (2016). Neutral point testing of color vision in the domestic cat. *Experimental Eye Research* 153, 23–6.

10. Ofri, R (Personal communication, 5 August 2022).

11. Ofri (2020).

12. Ibid.

13. Ibid.

14. Ibid.

15. Ofri (2008).

16. Ibid.

17. Ofri (2020).

18. Bartholomew, A (1582). *De Proprietatibus Rerum* Available at https://quod.lib.umich.edu/e/eebo/A05237.0001.001/1:29?rgn=div1;view=fulltext (last accessed 31 October 2022).

19. Xue, T, Do, M T H, Riccio, A, Jiang, Z, Hsieh, H, Wang, H C, Merbs, S L, Welsbie, D S, Yoshioka, T, Weissgerber, P, Stolz, S, Flockerzi, V, Freichel, M, Simon, M I, Clapham, D E and Yaw, K W (2011). Melanopsin signalling in mammalian iris and retina. *Nature* 479 (7371), 67–73.

20. Douglas, R H and Jeffery, G (2013). The spectral transmission of ocular media suggests ultraviolet sensitivity is widespread among mammals. *Proceedings of the Royal Society, B: Biological Sciences* 281 (1780), 20132995.

21. Ofri, R (Personal communication, 6 August 2022).

22. Ofri (2020).

23. Heffner, R S and Heffner, H E (1985). Hearing range of the domestic cat. *Hearing Research* 19, 85–8.

24. Ibid.

25. Ibid.

26. University of Sussex. Growling in domestic dogs. Available at www.lifesci.sussex. ac.uk/cmvcr/Growling_in_domestic_dogs.html. (last accessed 2 August 2022).

27. Populin, L C and Yin, T C T (1998). Behavioral studies of sound localization in the cat. *The Journal of Neuroscience* 18, 2147–60.

28. Heffner, H E and Heffner, R S (1998). Hearing. *Comparative Psychology, A Handbook*, ed. G Greenberg and M Haraway. New York: Garland, 290–303.

29. Ibid.

30. Fay, R and Popper, A N (2000). Evolution of hearing in vertebrates: the inner ears and processing. *Hearing Research* 149, 1–10.

31. Heffner, H E and Heffner, R S (1992). Auditory perception. *Farm Animals and the Environment*, ed. C Phillips and D Piggins. Wallingford: D A B International, 159–84.

CHAPTER FIVE:
WHAT YOU SMELL, TASTE AND TOUCH AS A CAT

1. Wyatt, T D (2014). *Pheromones and Animal Behavior: Chemical Signals and Signatures*, 2nd edn. Cambridge: Cambridge University Press.

2. Mayes, E-R E, Wilkinson, A, Pike, T W and Mills, D S (2015). Individual differences in visual and olfactory cue preference and use by cats (*Felis catus*). *Applied Animal Behaviour Science* 173, 52–9.

3. Nimura, Y (2012). Olfactory receptor multigene family in vertebrates: from the viewpoint of evolutionary genomics. *Current Genomics* 13, 103–14.

4. Laska, M (Personal communication, 2 December, 2021).

5. Haddon, C (1999). *The Daily Telegraph CAT Questions and Answers: Invaluable Advice for Cats and Their Owners*. London: Robinson/Daily Telegraph.

6. Bradshaw, J W S, Casey, R A and Brown S L (2012). *The Behaviour of the Domestic Cat*, 2nd edn. Wallingford: CABI.

7. Laska (2021).

8. Shreve, K R and Udell, M A R (2017). Stress, security and scent: the influence of chemical signals on the social life of domestic cats and implications for applied settings. *Applied Animal Behaviour Science* 187, 69–76.

9. Young, J M, Massa, H F, Hsu, L and Trask, B J (2010). Extreme variability among mammalian V1R gene families. *Genome Research* 20, 10–18.

10. Mills, D, Dube, M B and Zulch, H (2013). *Stress and Pheromonatherapy*, 2nd edn. Oxford: Wiley-Blackwell.

11. Beauchamp, G. and Jiang, P (2015). Comparative biology of taste: insights into mechanism and function. *Flavour* 4, 1–3.

12. Horwitz, D F, Soulard, Y and Junien-Castagna, A (2008). Factors affecting the feeding behavior of the cat. *Encyclopedia of Feline Clinical Nutrition*, ed. P Pibot, V Biourge and D A Elliot. Aimargues: Aniwa SAS.

13. Li, X, Li, W, Wang, H, Cao, J, Maehashi, K, Huang, L, Bachmanov, A, Reed, D R, Legrand-Defretin, V, Beauchamp, G K and Brand, J G (2005). Pseudogenization of a sweet-receptor gene accounts for cats' indifference toward sugar. *PloS Genetics* 1, e3.

14. Bradshaw, J W S, Goodwin, D, Legrand-Defretin, V and Nott, H M R (1996). Food selection by the domestic cat, an obligate carnivore. *Journal of Comparative Biochemical Physiology* 114, 205–9.

15. Aspinall, V and Cappello, M (2020). *Introduction to Animal and Veterinary Anatomy and Physiology*, 4th edn. Wallingford: CABI.

16. Lei, W, Ravoninjohary, A, Li, X, Margolskee, R F, Reed, D R, Beauchamp, G K and Jiang, P (2015). Functional analyses of bitter taste receptors in domestic cats (*Felis catus*). *PLOS One* 10, e0139670.

17. Laffitte, A (2022). Why are cats such fussy eaters? Available at https://www.linkedin.com/pulse/why-cats-fussy-eaters-anni-laffitte/ (last accessed 8 June 2022).

18. Ibid.

19. Bartoshuk, L M, Harned, M A and Parks, L H (1971). Taste of water in the cat: effects on sucrose preference. *Science* 171, 699–701.

20. Bradshaw, Casey, Brown (2012).

21. Rauscheker, J P, Tian, B, Korte, M and Egert, U (1993) Crossmodal changes in the somatosensory vibrissae/barrel system of visually deprived animals. *Proceedings of the National Academy of Sciences* 89, 5063–7.

22. Bradshaw, Casey, Brown (2012).

CHAPTER SIX:
HOW YOU TALK AS A CAT – WITH SOUND, BODY LANGUAGE AND TOUCH

1. Bradshaw, J W S, Casey, R A and Brown, S L (2012). *The Behaviour of the Domestic Cat*, 2nd edn. Wallingford: CABI.

2. Atkinson, T (2017). *Practical Feline Behaviour: Understanding Cat Behaviour and Improving Cat Welfare*. Wallingford: CABI.

3. Owens, J L, Olsen, M, Fontaine, A, Kloth, C, Kershenbaum, A and Waller, S (2017). Visual classification of feral cat *Felis silvestris catus* vocalisations. *Current Zoology* 63, 331–9.

4. Schötz, S (2022). Cat sounds: cat vocalisation types. *Melody in Human–Cat Communications (Meowsic)*. Available at http://meowsic.se (last accessed 1 July 2022).

5. Eklund, R, Peters, G and Duthie, E D (2010). An acoustic analysis of purring in the cheetah (*Acinonyx jubatus*) and in the domestic cat (*Felis catus*). *Fonetik 2010, Lund University, 2–4 June 2010, Lund, Sweden*, 17–22.

6. Tavernier, C, Ahmet, S, Houpts, K A and Yeon, S C (2020). Feline vocal communication. *Journal of Veterinary Science* 21, e18.

7. McComb, K, Taylor, A M, Wilson, C and Charlton, B D (2009). The cry embedded within the purr. *Current Biology* 19, R507–R508.

8. Tavernier et al. (2020).

9. Bradshaw, J (Personal communication 1 January, 2022).

10. Schotz, S, van der Weijer, J, Eklund, R (2019). Phonetic methods in cat vocalisations studies: a report from the Meowsic project. In *Proceedings from Fonetik*, 2019, 10–12.

11. Ellis, S L H, Swindell, V and Burmen, O H P (2015). Human classification of context-related vocalizations emitted by familiar and unfamiliar domestic cats: an exploratory study. *Anthrozoos* 28, 625–34.

12. BBC (2022). Pet cat missing for 10 years in Aberdeen reunited with owners. Available at www.bbc.co.uk/news/uk-scotland-north-east-orkney-shetland-58597174 (last accessed 29 April 2022).

13. Leyhausen, P (1979). *Cat Behavior: The Predatory and Social Behavior of Domestic and Wild Cats*. New York: Garland Publishing.

14. Ibid.

15. Bennett, V, Gourkow, N and Mills, D S (2017). Facial correlates of emotional behaviour in the domestic cat (*Felis catus*). *Behavioural Processes* 141, 342–50.

16. Humphrey, T, Proops, L, Forman, J, Spooner, R and McComb, K (2020). The role of cat eye narrowing movements in cat–human interaction communication. *Scientific Reports* 10, 1–8.

17. Kessler, M R and Turner, C C (1997). Stress and adaptation of cats (*Felis silvestris catus*) housed singly and in groups in boarding catteries. *Animal Welfare* 6, 243–54.

18. Crowell-Davis, S L, Curtis, T M and Knowles, R J (2003). Social organisation in the cat: a modern understanding. *Journal of Feline Medicine and Surgery* 6, 19–28.

19. Van den Bos, R (1998). The function of allogrooming in domestic cats (*Felis silvestris catus*): a study in a group of cats living in confinement. *Journal of Ethology* 16, 1.

20. Gajdoš-Kmecová, N, Petková, B, Kottferová, J, Halls, V, Haddon, C, Santos de Assis, L and Mills, D S (2022). Are these cats playing, fighting or is it something in between? Behavioural analysis of vigorous close contact intercat interactions. In press.

CHAPTER SEVEN:
HOW AS A CAT YOU TALK WITH SCENT –
YOUR SECRET LANGUAGE

1. Wyatt, T D (2014). *Pheromones and Animal Behavior: Chemical Signals and Signatures*, 2nd edn. Cambridge: Cambridge University Press.

2. Pageat, P (2003). Current research in canine and feline pheromones. *The Veterinary Clinics Small Animal Practice* 33, 187–311.

3. Ibid.

4. Ibid.

5. Ibid.

6. Shreve, K R and Udell, M A R (2017). Stress, security and scent: the influence of chemical signals on the social life of domestic cats and implications for applied settings. *Applied Animal Behaviour Science* 187, 69–76.

7. Ellis, S, Rodan, I, Carney, H C, Heath, S, Rochlitz, I, Shearburn, A D, Sundahl, E and Westropp, J L (2013). AAFP and ISFM Feline Environmental Needs Guidelines. *Journal of Feline Medicine and Surgery* 15, 219–30.

8. Hendriks, W H, Moughan, P J, Tarttelin, M F and Woolhouse, A D (1995). Felinine: a urinary amino acid of Felidae. *Comparative Biochemical Physiology* 112B, 581–8.

9. Suzuki, C, Miyazaki, T, Yamashita, T and Miyazaki, M (2019). GC× GC-MS-based volatile profiling of male domestic cat urine and the olfactory abilities of cats to discriminate temporal changes and individual differences in urine. *Journal of Chemical Ecology* 45, 579–87.

10. Feldman, H. (1994). Methods of scent marking in the domestic cat. *Canadian Journal of Zoology* 72, 1093–9.

11. Verbene, G. and de Boer, J. (1976). Chemocommunication among domestic cats, mediated by the olfactory and vomeronasal senses. *Zeitschrift für Tierpsychologie* 42, 8610R.

12. Feldman (1994).

13. Barcelos, A M, McPeake, K, Affenzeller, N and Mills, D S (2018). Common risk factors for urinary house soiling (periuria) in cats and its differentiation: the sensitivity and specificity of common diagnostic signs. *Frontiers in Veterinary Science* 5, 108.

14. Suzuki et al. (2019).

15. Miyazaki, T, Nishimura, T, Yamashita, T and Miyazaki, M (2018). Olfactory discrimination of anal sac secretions in the domestic cat and the chemical profiles of the volatile compounds. *Journal of Ethology* 36, 99–105.

16. Ibid.

17. Miyazaki, M, Miyazaki, T, Nishimura, T, Hojo, W and Yamashita, T (2018). The chemical basis of species, sex, and individual recognition using feces in the domestic cat. *Journal of Chemical Ecology* 44, 364–73.

18. Ibid.

19. Ishido, Y and Shimizu, M (1998). Influence of social rank on defecating behaviors in feral cats. *Journal of Ethology* 16, 15–21.

20. Kasbaoui, N, Bienboire-Frosini, C, Monneret, P, Leclercq, J, Descout, E, Cozzi, A and Pageat, P (2022). Influencing elimination location in the domestic cat: a semiochemical approach. *Animals* 12, 896.

21. Ellis, J J, McGowan, R T S and Martin, F (2017). Does previous use affect litter box appeal in multi-cat households? *Behavioural Processes*, 141, 284–90.

22. Wilson, C, Bain, M, DePorter, T, Beck, A, Grassi, V and Landsberg, G (2016). Owner observations regarding cat scratching behavior: an internet-based survey. *Journal of Feline Medicine and Surgery* 18:10, 791–7.

23. DePorter, T L and Elzerman, A L (2019). Common feline problem behaviors: destructive scratching. *Journal of Feline Medicine and Surgery* 21, 235–43.

24. Feldman (1994).

25. DePorter and Elzerman (2019).

CHAPTER EIGHT:
WHAT IT IS LIKE TO FEEL FELINE EMOTIONS

1. Barcelos, A M, McPeake, K, Affenzeller, N and Mills, D S (2018). Common risk factors for urinary house soiling (periuria) in cats and its differentiation: the sensitivity and specificity of common diagnostic signs. *Frontiers in Veterinary Science* 5, 108.

2. Panksepp, J and Watt, D (2011). What is basic about basic emotions? Lasting lessons from affective neuroscience. *Emotion Review* 3, 1–10.

3. Darwin, C (1872) *The Expression of Emotions in Man and Animals*, London, John Murray.

4. Morgan, C L (1903). *An Introduction to Comparative Psychology*, 2nd edn. London: W. Scott.

5. Skinner B F (1953). *Science and Human Behaviour*. New York: The Free Press.

6. Panksepp, J (2005). Affective consciousness: core emotional feelings in animals and humans. *Consciousness and Cognition* 14, 30–80.

7. Panksepp, J (2015).

8. Morris, P H, Doe, C and Godsell, E (2008). Secondary emotions in non-primate species? Behavioural reports and subjective claims by animal owners. *Cognition and Emotion* 22, 1–18.

9. Davis, K L and Montag, C (2019). Selected principles of Pankseppian affective neuroscience. *Frontiers in Neuroscience* 12, 1025.

10. Mills, D, Dube, M B and Zulch, H. (2013). *Stress and Pheromonatherapy in Small Animal Clinical Behaviour*. Chichester: Wiley-Blackwell.

11. Ibid.

12. McMillan, F D (2016). The psychobiology of social pain: evidence for a neurocognitive overlap with physical pain and welfare implications for social animals with special attention to the domestic dog (*Canis familiaris*). *Physiology and Behavior* 167, 154–71.

13. Scherer, K R (1984). On the nature and function of emotion: a component process approach. In *Approaches to Emotion*, ed. K R Scherer and P Ekman. New York: Psychology Press, 293–317.

14. Mendl, M and Harcourt, R (2003). Individuality in the domestic cat: origins, development and stability. In *The Domestic Cat: The Biology of Its Behaviour*, ed. D C Turner and P Bateson, 2nd edn. Cambridge: Cambridge University Press, 48–64.

15. Arahori, M, Hori, Y, Saito, A, Chijiiwa, H, Takagi, S, Ito, Y, Watanabe, A, Inoue-Murayama, M and Fujita, K (2016). The oxytocin receptor gene *(OXTR)* polymorphism in cats (*Felis catus*) is associated with 'roughness' assessed by owners. *Journal of Veterinary Behavior* 11, 109–12.

16. Davis and Montag (2019).

17. Skinner (1984).

CHAPTER NINE:
WHAT IT IS LIKE TO THINK AS A CAT

1. Shettleworth, S J (2000). Modularity and the evolution of cognition. In *The Evolution of Cognition*, ed. C M Heyes and L Huber. Cambridge, MA: MIT Press, 43–60.

2. Brauer, J, Hanus, D, Pika, S, Gray, R and Uomini, N (2020). Old and new approaches to animal cognition: there is not 'one cognition'. *Journal of Intelligence* 8, 28.

3. Dumas, C (1992). Object permanence in cats (*Felis catus*): an ecological approach to the study of invisible displacements. *Journal of Comparative Psychology* 106, 404–10.

4. Ibid.

5. Bateson, P and Turner, D (2000). Questions about cats. In *The Domestic Cat: The Biology of Its Behaviour*, ed. D C Turner and P Bateson, 2nd edn. Cambridge: Cambridge University Press, 230–7.

6. Thorndike, E L (1911). *Animal Intelligence*. New York: The Macmillan Company.

7. Jaroš, P (2017). The three semiotic lives of domestic cats: a case study on animal social cognition. *Biosemiotics* 110, 270–93.

8. Quoted in Sorabji, R (2018). Augustine on irrational animals and the Christian tradition. In *Animal Minds and Human Morals: The Origins of the Western Debate*. Ithaca, NY: Cornell University Press, 195–207.

9. Jaroš (2017).

10. Saito, A, Shinozuka, K, Ito, Y and Hasegawa, T (2019). Domestic cats *(Felis catus)* discriminate their names from other words. *Scientific Reports* 9, 1–8.

11. Saito, A and Shinozuka, K (2013). Vocal recognition of owners by domestic cats (*Felis catus*). *Animal Cognition* 16, 685–90.

12. Ibid.

13. Tagaki, S, Saito, A, Arahori, M, Chijiiwa, H, Koyasu, H, Nagasawa, M, Kikusui, T, Fujita, K and Kuroshima, H (2022). Cats learn the names of their friend cats in their daily lives. *Scientific Reports* 12, 1–9.

14. Sherman, B L, Gruen, M E, Meeker, R B, Milgram, B, DiRivera, C, Thomson, A, Clary, G and Hudson, L (2013). The use of a T-maze to measure cognitive-motor function in cats. *Journal of Veterinary Behavior* 8, 32–9.

15. Ibid.

16. Hippisley Coxe, A D (1951). *A Seat at the Circus*. London: Evans Brothers.

17. Bradshaw, J H and Ellis, S (2016). *The Trainable Cat: How to Make Life Happier for You and Your Cat*. London: Allen Lane.

18. Vitale Shreve, K R and Udell, M A R (2015). What's inside your cat's head? A review of cat (*Felis silvestris catus*) cognition research past, present and future. *Animal Cognition* 18, 1195–206.

19. Szenczi, P, Urrutia, A, Hudson, R and Banszegim, O (2021). Are you my mummy? Long-term olfactory memory of mother's body odour by offspring in the domestic cat. *Animal Cognition* 25, 21–6.

20. Suddendorf, T. and Corbalis, M C (2010). Behavioural evidence for mental time travel in nonhuman animals. *Behavioural Brain Research* 215, 292–8.

21. Healey, K, McNally, L, Ruxton, G D, Cooper, N and Jackson, A L (2013). Metabolic rate and body size are linked with perception of temporal information. *Animal Behaviour* 86, 685–69.

22. Modra, G, Maak, I, Lorincz, A, Juhasz, O, Kiss, P J and Lorinczi, G (2020). Protective behavior or 'true' tool use? Scrutinizing the tool use behavior of ants. *Ecology and Evolution* 10, 13787–95.

23. Pisa, P E and Agrillo, C (2009). Quantity discrimination in felines: a preliminary investigation of the domestic cat *(Felis silvestris catus)*. *Journal of Ethology* 27, 289–93.

24. Quarantia, A, d'Ingeo, S, Amoruso, R and Siniscalchi, M (2020). Emotion recognition in cats. *Animals* 10, 1107.

25. Wynne, C D L (2004). *Do Animals Think?* Princeton, NJ: Princeton University Press.

26. Ibid.

27. Ibid.

CHAPTER TEN:
WHAT IT IS LIKE BEING A RESCUE CAT

1. McDonald, J L and Skilling, E (2021). Human influences shape the first spatially explicit national estimate of urban unowned cat abundance. *Scientific Reports* 11, 1–12.

2. Clark, C C, Gruffydd-Jones, T and Murray, J K (2012). Number of cats and dogs in UK welfare organisations. *Veterinary Record* 170, 493.

3. Animal Medicines Australia (2022). Pets and the pandemic: A social research snapshot of pets and people in the COVID-19 era. Available at https://animalmedicinesaustralia.org.au/report/pets-and-the-pandemic-a-social-research-snapshot-of-pets-and-people-in-the-covid-19-era-2/ (last accessed 27 October 2022).

4. Invasive Species Council (2022). Available at https://invasives.org.au/our-work/feral-animals/cats-in-australia/ (last accessed 27 October 2022).

5. AVMA (2022). U.S. pet ownership statistics. Available at www.avma.org/resources-tools/reports-statistics/us-pet-ownership-statistics (last accessed 27 October 2022).

6. American Humane Society (2022). Outdoor Cats FAQ. Available at https://www.humanesociety.org/resources/outdoor-cats-faq (last accessed 27 October 2022).

7. iCatCare (2022a). iCatCare-2020-Annual Report. Available at https://icatcare.org/icatcare-publishes-2020-annual-report/ (last accessed 28 April 2022).

8. ISFM (2013). ISFM guidelines on population management and welfare of unowned domestic cats (*Felis catus*). *Journal of Feline Medicine and Surgery* 15, 811–17.

9. Australian Government (2022). Feral cats. Available at https://www.dcceew.gov.au/environment/biodiversity/threatened/publications/factsheet-tackling-feral-cats-and-their-impacts-faqs (last accessed 22 July 2022).

10. Robertson, S A (2008). A review of feral cat control. *Journal of Feline Medicine and Surgery* 10, 366–75.

11. Ibid.

12. Spehar, D D and Wolf, P J (2017). An examination of an iconic Trap-Neuter-Return Program: The Newburyport, Massachusetts Case Study. *Animals* 7, 81.

13. Alger, J M and Alger, S F (2003). *Cat Culture: The Social World of a Cat Shelter*. Philadelphia: Temple University Press.

14. Finka, L (Personal communication 20 July 2022).

15. Halls, V (Personal communication 29 April 2022).

16. Wells, E (Personal communication 22 June 2022).

17. iCatCare (2022b). Cat-friendly homing – what is an in-betweener? Available at https://icatcare.org/cat-friendly-homing-what-is-an-inbetweener/ (last accessed 27 April 2022).

18. Gourkow, N and Fraser, D (2006). The effect of housing and handling practices on the welfare, behaviour and selection of domestic cats *(Felis sylvestris catus)* by adopters in an animal shelter. *Animal Welfare* 15, 371–7.

19. BBC (2022). Pet cat missing for 10 years in Aberdeen reunited with owners. Available at: https://www.bbc.co.uk/news/uk-scotland-north-east-orkney-shetland-58597174 (last accessed 29 April 2022).

20. BBC (2013). Crunchy's Animal Rescue staff convicted of cruelty. Available at https://www.bbc.co.uk/news/uk-england-oxfordshire-23032419 (last accessed 17 July 2022).

21. Halls, V (personal communication, 29 April 2022).

22. iCatCare (2022a). Cat friendly homing. Available at https://icatcare.org/unowned-cats/cat-friendly-homing/ (last accessed 30 April 2022).

23. Wagner, D, Hurley, K and Stavisky, J (2018). Principles of design for health, welfare and rehoming. *Journal of Feline Medicine and Surgery* 20, 635–42.

24. Suarez, P, Recuerda, P.and Arias-de-Reyna, L (2017). Behaviour and welfare: the visitor effect in captive felids. *Animal Welfare* 26, 25–34.

25. Kogan, L, Kolus, C and Schoenfeld-Tacher, R (2017). Assessment of clicker training for shelter cats. *Animals* 7, 73.

26. Kessler, M R and Turner, D C (1997). Stress and adaptation of cats housed singly, in pairs and in groups in boarding catteries. *Animal Welfare* 6, 243–54.

27. Gouveia, K, Magalhães, K and de Sousa, L (2011). The behaviour of domestic cats in a shelter: residence time, density and sex ratio. *Applied Animal Behaviour Science* 130, 53–9.

28. Stella, J L, Lord, L K and Buffington, C A T (2013). Sickness behaviors in response to unusual external events in healthy cats and cats with interstitial cystitis. *JAVMA* 238, 67–73.

29. American Humane (2022). Animal shelter euthanasia. Available at https://www.americanhumane.org/fact-sheet/animal-shelter-euthanasia/ (last accessed 30 April 2022).

30. Alberthsen, C, Rand. J S, Bennett, P C, Paterson, M, Lawrie, M and Morton, J M (2013). Cat admissions to RSPCA shelters in Queensland, Australia: description of cats and risk factor for euthanasia after entry. *Australian Veterinary Journal* 91, 35–42.

31. Kerr, C A, Rand, J, Morton, J M, Reid, R and Paterson, M (2018). Changes associated with improved outcomes for cats entering RSPCA Queensland shelters from 2011 to 2016. *Animals* 8, 95.

32. Stavisky, J, Brennan, M L, Downes, M and Dean, R (2012). Demographics and economic burden of un-owned cats and dogs in the UK: results of a 2010 census. *BMC Veterinary Research* 8, 1–10.

33. Feighelstein, M, Shimshoni, I, Finka, L R, Luna, S P, Mills, D S and Zamansky, A. (2022). Automated recognition of pain in cats. *Scientific Reports* 12, 1–10.

34. Université de Montréal (2019). *Feline Grimace Scale* app. Available at https://www.felinegrimacescale.com/phone-app (last accessed 6 July 2022).

CHAPTER ELEVEN:
WHAT IT IS LIKE BEING A PET

1. Zasloff, R L (1996). Measuring attachment to companion animals: a dog is not a cat is not a bird. *Applied Animal Behaviour Science* 47, 43–8.
2. Qureshi, A I, Memon, M Z, Vazquez, G and Suri, M F K (2009). Cat ownership and the risk of fatal cardiovascular diseases: results from the Second National Health and Nutrition Examination Study Mortality Follow-up Study. *Journal of Vascular and Interventional Neurology*, 2, 132–5.
3. Ines, M, Ricci-Bonot, C and Mills, D S (2021). My cat and me – a study of cat owner perceptions of their bond and relationship. *Animals* 11, 1601.
4. Ellis, S L H, Rodan, I, Carney, H C, Heath, S, Rochlitz, I, Shearburn, L D, Sundah, E and Westropp, J L (2013). AAFT and ISFM Feline Environmental Needs Guidelines. *Journal of Feline Medicine and Surgery* 15, 219–30.
5. Koolhas, J M (2008). Coping style and immunity in animals: making sense of individual variation. *Brain, Behavior, and Immunity*, 22, 662–7.
6. Mills, D, Karagiannis, C and Zulch, H (2014). Stress – its effects on health and behavior: a guide for practitioners. *Veterinary Clinics Small Animal Practice* 44, 525–41.
7. Mariti, C, Guerrini, F, Vallini, V, Bowen, J E, Fatjo, J, Diverio, S, Sighieri, C and Gazzano, A. (2017). The perception of cat stress by Italian owners. *Journal of Veterinary Behavior*, 20, 74–81.
8. Carlstead, K, Brown, J L and Strawn, W (1993). Behavioral and physiological correlates of stress in laboratory cats. *Applied Animal Behaviour Science* 38, 143–58.
9. Shreve, K R and Udell, M A R (2017). Stress, security and scent: the influence of chemical signals on the social life of domestic cats and implications for applied settings. *Applied Animal Behaviour Science*, 187, 69–76.
10. UK Petfood (2022). Cat nutrition. Available at https://www.ukpetfood.org/information-centre/pet-nutrition-hub/cat-nutrition.html (last accessed December 13 2022).
11. Fitzgerald, B M and Turner, D C (2000). Hunting behaviour of domestic cats and their impact on prey populations. *The Domestic Cat: The Biology of Its Behaviour*, ed. D C Turner and P Bateson, 2nd edn. Cambridge: Cambridge University Press, 151–79.
12. Handl, S and Fritz, J (2022). The water requirements and drinking habits of cats. *Veterinary Focus* 28.3. Available at https://vetfocus.royalcanin.com/en/

scientific/the-water-requirements-and-drinking-habits-of-cats (last accessed 7 April 2022).

13. O'Neill, D G, Church, D B, McGreevy, P D, Thomson, P C and Brodbelt, D C (2015). Longevity and mortality of cats attending primary care veterinary practices in England. *Journal of Feline Medicine and Surgery* 17, 125–33.

14. Chalkowski, K, Wilson, A E, Lepczyk, C A and Zohdy, S (2018). Who let the cats out? A global meta-analysis on risk of parasitic infection in indoor versus outdoor domestic cats (*Felis catus*). *Biology Letters* 15, 20180840.

15. Cecchetti, M, Crowley, S L, Goodwin, C E D and McDonald, R A (2021). Provision of high meat content food and object play reduce the predation of wild animals by domestic cats, *Felis catus*. *Current Biology* 31, 1107–11.

16. Assis, L S de and Mills, D S (2021). Introducing a controlled outdoor environment impacts positively in cat welfare and owner concerns: the use of a new feline welfare assessment tool. *Frontiers in Veterinary Science* 7, 599284.

17. McMillan, F D (2012). Stress-induced and emotional eating in animals: a review of the experimental evidence and implications for companion animals. *Journal of Veterinary Behavior* 8, 376–85.

18. Sandøe, P, Nørspang, A P, Forkman, B, Bjørnvad, C R, Kondrug, S V and Lund, T B (2017). The burden of domestication: a representative study of welfare in privately owned cats in Denmark. *Animal Welfare* 26, 1–10.

19. Finka, L and Foreman-Worsley, R (2011). Are multi-cat homes more stressful? A critical review of the evidence associated with cat group size and wellbeing. *Journal of Feline Medicine and Surgery* 24, 65–76.

20. Ramos, D (2019). Common feline problem behaviors: aggression in multi-cat households. *Journal of Feline Medicine and Surgery*, 21, 221–33.

21. Heath, S (2016). Intercat conflict. *Feline Behavioral Health and Welfare*, ed. S Heath and I Rodan. St Louis, MO: Elsevier, 357–73.

22. Ibid.

23. Elzerman, A L, DePorter, T L, Beck, A and Collin, J-F (2020). Conflict and affiliative behavior frequency between cats in multi-cat households: a survey-based study. *Journal of Feline Medicine and Surgery* 22, 705–17.

24. Heath (2016).

25. Ramos, D, Arena M N, Reche-Junior, A, Daniel, A G T, Albino, M V C, Vasconcellos, A S, Viau, P and Oliviera, C A (2012). Factors affecting faecal glucocorticoid levels in domestic cats (*Felis catus*): a pilot study with single and large multi-cat households. *Animal Welfare* 21, 285–91.

26. Koyasu, H and Nagasawa, M (2019). Recognition of directed-gaze from humans by cats. *Japanese Journal of Animal Psychology* 69, 27–34.

27. Ramos, D, Reche-Junior, A, Fragoso, P L, Palme, R, Yanasse, N K, Gouvea, V R, Beck, A and Mills, D S (2013). Are cats (*Felis catus*) from multi-cat households

more stressed? Evidence from assessment of fecal glucocorticoid metabolite analysis. *Physiology and Behavior* 122, 72–5.

28. Ramos, D and Mills, D S (2009). Human-directed aggression in Brazilian domestic cats, owner-reported prevalence, contexts and risk factors. *Journal of Feline Medicine and Surgery* 11, 835–41.

29. Ellis, S L H, Thompson, H, Guijarro, C and Zulch, H E (2015). The influence of body region, handler familiarity and order of region handled on the domestic cat's response to being stroked. *Applied Animal Behaviour Science* 173, 60–7.

30. Turner, D C (2021). Unanswered questions and hypotheses about domestic cat behavior, ecology, and the cat–human relationship. *Animals* 11, 2823.

CHAPTER TWELVE:
WHAT YOU AS A CAT WANT – CHOICE AND CONTROL

1. Cats Protection (2022). Kitten socialisation. Available at https://www.cats.org.uk/help-and-advice/pregnancy-and-kitten-care/kitten-socialisation (last accessed 9 August 2022).

2. Joyce, A and Yates, D (2011). Help stop teenage pregnancy: early neutering in cats. *Journal of Feline Medicine and Surgery* 13, 3–10.

3. Finka, L R, Ripari, L, Quinlan, L, Haywood, C, Puzzo, J, Jordan, A, Tsui, J, Foreman-Worsley, R, Dixon, L and Brennan, M L (2022). Investigation of human individual differences as predictors of their animal interaction styles, focused on the domestic cat. *Scientific Reports* 12, 1–13.

4. Haddon, C (2022). Meow too: has your cat consented to petting? Available at https://www.youtube.com/watch?v=8FVPtQcjKvs (last accessed 5 April 2022).

5. Cats Protection (2022). Getting another cat. Available at https://www.cats.org.uk/help-and-advice/cats-and-your-family/other-cats (last accessed 9 August 2022).

6. Cats Protection (2022). Dogs and other pets. Available at https://www.cats.org.uk/help-and-advice/cats-and-your-family/dogs-and-other-pets (last accessed 9 August 2022).

APPENDIX

1. Turner, D C (2021). Unanswered questions and hypotheses about domestic cat behavior, ecology, and the cat–human relationship. *Animals* 11, 2823.

2. Koyasu, H and Nagasawa, M (2019). Recognition of directed-gaze from humans by cats. *Japanese Journal of Animal Psychology* 69, 27–34.

3. Handl, S and Fritz, J (2022). The water requirements and drinking habits of cats. *Veterinary Focus* 28.3. Available at https://vetfocus.royalcanin.com/en/scientific/the-water-requirements-and-drinking-habits-of-cats (last accessed 7 April 2022).

4. Ibid.

5. Robbins, M T, Cline, M G, Bartges, J W, Felty E, Saker, K E, Bastian, R and Witzel, A L (2019). Quantified water intake in lab cats from still, free falling and circulation water bowls and its effect on selected urinary parameters. *Journal of Feline Medicine and Surgery* 21, 682–90.

6. Handl and Fritz (2022).

7. Wooding, B and Mills, D S (2007). Drinking water preferences in the cat. *Journal of Veterinary Behavior* 2, 87.

8. Yeomans, J S and Frankland, P W (1996). The acoustic startle reflex: neurons and connections. *Brain Research Reviews* 21, 301–14.

9. Cecchetti, M, Crowley, S L, McDonald, J and McDonald, R A (2022). Owner-ascribed personality profiles distinguish domestic cats that capture and bring home wild animal prey. *Applied Animal Behaviour Science*, 105774.

10. Cecchetti, M, Crowley, S L, Goodwin, C E D and McDonald, R A (2021). Provision of high meat content food and object play reduce the predation of wild animals by domestic cats, *Felis catus*. *Current Biology* 31, 1107–11.

11. Ofri, R (2008). Vision in the animal kingdom. *Proceedings of the 33rd World Small Animal Veterinary Congress*, 242–4.

12. Heffner, R S and Heffner, H E (1985). Hearing range of the domestic cat. *Hearing Research* 19, 85–8.

13. Kry, K and Casey, R (2007). The effect of hiding enrichment on stress levels and the behaviour of domestic cats (*Felis sylvestris catus*) in a shelter setting and the implications for adoption potential. *Animal Welfare* 16, 375–83.

14. Smith, G E, Chouinard, P A and Byosiere, S E (2021). If I fits I sits: a citizen science investigation into illusory contour susceptibility in domestic cats (*Felis sylvestris catus*). *Applied Animal Behaviour Science* 240, 105338.

INDEX

A
Abyssinian kittens 50
Actinidia kolomikta 91
action tendency 149
adoption 174, 180, 183, 184, 210
African wildcat 35, 38, 39–40, 46, 47
agility 16–20
allogrooming 117
American Association of Feline
    Practitioners 188
Americas, arrival of domestic cats in 45
anal sac odour 129–31
ancestors 31–47
Animal Welfare Act (2006) 188
anthropomorphism 9–11, 137
anxiety 150, 200
Aphaenogaster ants 166
arachidonic acid 193
arginine 193
Aristophanes 45
attention, seeking 217–18
audiographs 104
Augustine of Hippo 157
Australia 45, 173, 188, 208
automatic physiological reactions 148–9
autonoetic consciousness 143
awareness, self- 168
awn hairs 98

B
balance 23, 24, 57, 113
Barnaby (cat) 107
Bastet 43, 44
Bateson, Patrick 155
bats 5–6, 78, 160
Beauchamp, Dr Gary 95
behaviour 6–7, 149, 207
    domesticated cats vs African wildcats 47
    learned 7
    normal feline 195–8
    pedigree breeds 50–1
    punishment for 210
behaviourism 139–41
bellies, exposing 109
big cats 103–4, 120

biological significance 81
biting 117, 118
blind cats 100
body language 108–10, 117, 118, 138, 157,
    207
body posture 113–15
body temperature 28, 29, 98
bonds 187, 198
bones 14–15, 17, 22
boredom 196, 197–8, 208
boxes, fascination with 219–20
Bradshaw, Dr John 99, 106
the brain 25, 136–7, 142
breeding: African wildcats 39
    domesticated and wild cats 46
    litters 37, 49
    lust system 146
    sexual development 63
British Isles, arrival of domestic
    cats 45
Bubastis 43–4
bunting 116, 123
burials, cat 41–2

C
care emotion 146
carpal hairs 100
carpal/stopper pad 17, 19
cat bells 217
cat consent test 207
cat flaps 192, 196–7, 207, 208
cat haters 213–14
caterwauls 107–8
CatFACS 111
catnip 91
Cats Protection 206
character 150
chirrup 106
cilia 24
civets 33
claws 15, 20–1
    declawing 131
    dew claws 15, 19
    kittens' 58
    kneading 116

claws – *cont'd.*
  nerve ends 99
  scratching and 131
climbing 58, 195–6
cognition 153–69
colostrum 54
combat, cat 108
communication 103–18, 157–8
  African wildcats 39
  body language 108–10, 117, 118, 157
  body posture 113–15
  facial expressions 110–12
  faeces system 129–31
  language of friendship 115–17
  scratching 131
  tails 112–13
  use of distance 115
  vocalizations 103–8, 118, 157
  with scent 88, 119–32
community cats 172, 177–86
  euthanasia 184–6
  rescue shelters 178–83
companionship 198–201
conflict 198, 200–1
consciousness 8–9, 137, 142
counting 166
Coxe, Antony Hippisley 162
critical anthropomorphism 11
cruelty, cat 44–5
cucumber 215–16
cuddling cats 202–3, 206
curfews 197
cutaneous marginal pouch 24
Cyprus 41–2
cystitis 135, 189, 195

D
Darwin, Charles 14, 138–9
Descartes, René 138
desire-wanting system 144
developmental delay 52
dew claws 15, 19
diet 193–5
digestive tract 26
digitigrade stance 17
diseases 50–1, 206
distance, use of 115
DNA 50–1
dogs 36, 46, 47

breeding 51
  and cats 138, 144, 209
  facial expressions 110–11
  genes 93, 150
  motivation 156
  noses 92
  raised paws 114
  scent 85–6, 90
  taste buds 96
  theory of mind 154, 167
domestication 35–47
Dominique and His Flying House
    Cats 162–3
drinking 27, 214–15
Duammeres 43

E
ears: detecting direction 79–81
  ear furnishings 29
  hearing 77–83
  Henry's pocket 24
  movement of 24, 80, 111
  range of hearing 78–9, 81–2
  sense and sensitivity 82–3
  ultrasonic noises 78–80, 83
  vestibular apparatus 24, 57
Egypt, ancient 42–5
emotions 10, 135–51
  body language and 109
  body posture and 114–15
  development of 148–50
  ear movement and 111
  emotional networks 143–7
  moods and temperaments 150–1
empathy 9, 11
ethology 141–3
European wild cat 35
euthanasia 184–6
evolution of the cat 31–47
eye contact 111–12, 201, 213
eyes 25
  blinking 112
  colour 72–3
  cones 73
  cornea 74
  development of 57
  and emotions 111
  flicker factor 76–7
  focus 80–1

iris 76
nictating membrane 75
night and twilight 74–6
pupils 74–5, 111
rods 75
tapetum lucidum 75–6
ultraviolet (UV) light 76
vision 67–77
visual field 71–2
whiskers above 100

F
facial expressions 110–12
facial marking 122–5
faeces 198
   buried vs unburied 129–31
   kittens 53, 58
   litter trays 192–3
falls 23–4
fat cats 195, 197
fear 60, 100, 107, 137, 150, 151
   body posture and 113, 114
   of cucumbers 215–16
   ear movement and 111
   emotional reaction 148–9
   fear-anxiety 145
   tails and 113
   training with 162
feelings, inner 149
Feline Grimace Scale 185
felinine 125–6
Felis lunensis 35
   F. silvestris catus 35–6
   F. s. lybica 37–8, 40–7, 104
feral cats 35, 46–7, 172–7
   cat sanctuaries 176–7
   developmental delay 52
   eliminating 173–4
   hunting 144
   kittens 60, 62
   meows 106
   pregnancies 64
   sensitive period 60, 62
   social maturity 65
   taming 62
   Trap, Neuter and Return programmes
      (TNR) 174–5, 177, 178
Fertile Crescent 40–1, 45
fighting 118, 198, 199, 200–1

Filhol, Henri 32
Finka, Dr Lauren 176–7
five pillars of feline bliss 188–9
flehmen response 94
flexibility 22
flicker factor 76–7
fMRI scans 142
food 53, 97, 193–5
Forbes (cat) 178–9
forelimbs 15, 17, 21
fossils, feline 32–5
frantic random activity periods 217–18
friendship, language of 115–17
frustration-rage 144–5, 146
fur coats 27–30
   and body temperature 98
   colour of 37–8
   grooming 26, 27, 28, 29
   matting of 29
   types of body hair 29, 98–9

G
gait 18
geckoes 23
genes 49–50, 61, 150–1
   scenting abilities 89
   taste 96, 97
   vomeronasal organ 93
grooming 26, 27, 28, 29
   allogrooming 117
   flexibility and 22
   overgrooming 196
   scent marks 123
growls 108
guard hairs 29, 98

H
'hairless' breeds 28–9, 99
Halls, Vicky 177, 179
hand-reared kittens 54–5
head shape 25
health benefits of owning a cat 187
hearing 77–83
   biological significance 81
   detecting direction 79–81
   development of 57
   range of hearing 78–9, 81–2
   sense and sensitivity 82–3
   ultrasonic noises 78–80, 83, 219

Henry's pocket 24
Herbst, Marna 39–40
Herodotus 44
hiding places 190–1
hindlegs 17, 18, 21
hissing 108, 199
homes, cat-friendly 178–83,
    188, 190
hormones, emotions and 149
horses 28, 71–2, 167
hunting 36, 144, 195–6
    bringing prey to humans 216–17
    in the dark 75
    and hearing 79, 82
    hunting instinct 160–1
    indoor-only cats 197
    kittens 52, 53, 58–9, 64–5
    object permanence 154–5
    pouncing 21
    and sense of smell 87–8, 91
    stalking 16
    vision and 70–2, 73
    whiskers and 100

I
imitation 155
inbetweeners 178
individuality 49–65, 89
indoor-only cats 192, 197, 208–9
    hunting 36
    litter trays 207–8
    play 208–9
    vaccinations 206
inner lives 8–11
intelligence, indicators of 165–8
International Cat Care 177,
    178, 179
International Commission on Zoological
    Nomenclature 35
International Society for Feline Medicine
    (ISFM) 172, 188
Ipuy 43
Iron Age 45

J
Jacobson's organ 93–4
Jaroš, Filip 156
jaws 25–6
jumps 21

K
Kanizsa square illusion 220
Kgalagadi Transfrontier Park
    39–40
kittens 49–65
    allogrooming 117
    balance 57
    care emotion 146
    carrying 166
    chirrups 106
    claws 58
    development of senses 56–7
    fathers of litters 49
    feral and wild cats 37, 52, 60, 62
    first few weeks 53–7
    food preferences 53, 58
    growth 58
    hand-reared 54–5
    handling 61, 206
    hunting skills 52, 53, 58–9, 64–5
    indoor-only cats 208
    juvenile period 62–5
    kneading 116
    maternal care 135, 137
    maturity 65
    meows 106, 107
    movement 57–8
    panic-grief 145
    pheromones 94, 133
    play 59, 63, 146, 197–8
    prenatal development 52–3, 56
    purring 105
    sensitive period 59–62
    sexual development 63
    shared nursing 156, 158
    sociability 59, 61, 62
    stress and 52
    teeth 58, 64
    urination and defecation 53, 58
    weaning 55–6, 58, 59
kneading 116–17
kokumi flavour 97

L
language 157
Laska, Matthias 89, 92–3
learning 160–5
LeFort, Dominique 162–3
legs 14–20, 21

lifespan 165
litter trays 58, 192–3, 198
  indoor-only cats 207–8
  location of 82–3, 181
  multi-cat households 128,
    130–1, 210
  scent 86, 129, 130–1
  zoomies after 218
litters 37
lust system 146
lynx tipping 29

M
Maine Coon 23
Malebranche, Nicolas 8
Manx cats 22, 24, 112
mating 37, 39, 49, 63
maturity 65
maze tests 161–2
mealtimes 10
mechanoreceptors 99
memory 163–5
mental mapping 164
meowing 106–7, 131, 163
Meowsic 104
metacarpal bones 17
mice 45, 78, 87, 91, 93
microchipping 206
Miocene 33
MMB 130
moods 150–1
moon walking 16
Morgan, Conwy Lloyd 6
Morgan's Canon 6, 139
mothering styles 53–4
motivation 156
  motivational level 80
  motivational tendency 149
movement, vision and 70–2, 73,
    218–19
mowls 107–8
mummified cats 44–5

N
Nagel, Thomas 5–7
nails, human 20–1
names, recognition of 158–9
Natufians 40–1
nature and nurture 49–53

Neolithic sites 41–2
neuroanatomical features 93
neuroscience 8–9, 10
neutering 63–4, 206
New Zealand 208
nictating membrane 75
night and twilight 74–6, 88, 100
nipping 117–18
Norwegian Forest kittens 50
noses 92–5

O
obesity 195, 197
object permanence 154–5
odours *see* scent and smelling
Ofri, Ron 72, 76
olfactory bulb 25
Oligocene epoch 31
Oriental kittens 50
overeating 197
overfeeding 194–5
ovulation 37
oxytocin 150

P
pads 17–19, 28, 202
pain 147, 151, 162, 185
panic-grief 145–6
Panksepp, Jaak 141
panting 28
papillae 27
parasites 197
patrolling 190, 196
paws 15, 20
  pads 17–20, 28, 202
  pheromone glands 122
  raised 114
  sensitivity of 99
pedigree breeds 210
  behaviour 50–1
  coat colour 38
  DNA 50
  health 50–1
  inbreeding 50–1
  sociability 51
Persians 51
personality 51, 150–1
PET scans 142
pets, life as 187–203

petting 202–3, 206–7, 213
  petting and biting
    syndrome 202
pheromones 94–5
  MMB 130
  pheromone mixtures
    121, 122
  scent marks 120
  scratching and 132
  spray marking 127–8
Phoenicians 45
pinnae 24
plantigrade posture 185
play 63, 208–9, 218
  indoor-only cats 197–8
  kittens 59
  object play 59
  rough-and-tumble play 117, 147
  social play 146–7
  subject play 59
polar bears 28
polydactyl cats 19–20
positive reinforcement 210
pouncing 21, 160
predictability 190–3, 200
preferred associates 173
pregnancy, unplanned 63
prenatal development 52–3, 56
prey: bringing to humans 216–17
  hunter stalking 16
  hunting instinct 160–1
  locating 24
  object permanence 154–5
  vision and 70–2, 73
  see also hunting
Proailurus 31–2
  P. lemanensis 32–3
Pseudaelurus 33
punishments 210
purring 104–6

Q
quality of life 186
quarantine 180

R
r-strategy 37
rabbits 28, 74, 120
rats 7, 52, 53–4, 58, 77, 81–2, 120

rescue cats 171–86
rescue shelters 178–83, 184–6
respiratory infections 95, 180, 183
roaring 104
rolling over 109–10
Romanes, George 139
Romans 45–6
routine 191, 201
Royal Society for Prevention of Cruelty to
    Animals (RSPCA) 178, 184
rubbing 116

S
sabre-toothed tigers 33–4
saliva 27, 28, 123
sanctuaries, cat 176–7
scents and smelling 2, 85–95
  cat shelters 181
  communicating with 119–32
  development of sense of smell 57
  family scent profile 86, 124, 133,
    191–2, 201, 214
  food 56
  how good is a cat's sense of 92–5
  and hunting 87–8, 91
  mice 87, 91
  mother's 56–7
  olfactory bulb 25
  scent marks 119–32, 157, 168, 198
  scent reassurance 132–3
  scratching and 132
  and sense of security 191–2
  signature scents 88, 121, 122–3
  smellscapes 2, 85–8, 95
  and taste 95
Schotz, Dr Susanne 104, 106–7
Scottish Society for Prevention of Cruelty to
    Animals (SSPCA) 178
Scottish wildcat 38
scratching 21, 117, 118, 131–2, 195–6, 198
security 190–3, 200, 219
self-awareness 143, 168
senses: development of 56–7
  see also hearing; sight, *etc*
sensitive period 59–62
sex 37, 94, 107
Shillourokambos 41–2
Siamese cats 50, 106
Siege of Paris (1870–71) 42

sight 67–77
  colour 72–3
  flicker factor 76–7
  focus 80–1
  night and twilight 74–6
similarity sandwich 168–9
skeleton 14–15
skin cancer 29
Skinner, B F 7–8, 139–40, 141
skulls, shape of 25
sleeping with humans 116
smell *see* scent and smelling
Smilodon 33
  S. populator 34
sniffing 123–4
sociability 199
  domesticated cats 47
  feral cats 46–7
  introducing new cats 201, 209
  kittens 59, 61, 62
  number of cats in a household
    209–10
  pedigree breeds 51
  relationships with other cats 115–17, 199,
    200
  signature scents 88
  social affiliation 146–7
  social bonds 117
  social odours 94
social intelligence hypothesis 156
social referencing period 62–5
social repulsion 147
social rolls 109–10
sounds 77–83
  communication 103
  detecting direction 79–81
  range of hearing 78–9, 81–2
  sense and sensitivity 82–3
  ultrasonic noises 78–80, 83, 219
space, respecting a cat's 206
sparrows 40–1, 45
Sphynx 28, 29
spine 22
spitting 199
spray marking 39, 64, 126–9
stalking 16
staring 111–12, 213
startle reflex 215–16
Stenogale 32

stray cats 64, 171–86
street cats 172, 177–86
stress 52, 54, 105, 189, 201
  body posture and 15, 114
  chronic stress 189, 191
  petting and 202
  rescue shelters 182, 183
  stress hormones 52
  unpredictability 190, 191, 200
stretching 13
stroking 202, 206–7
sun burn 29
sweating 28

T
tails 22–4
  balance and 113
  bones in 22
  communicating with 112–13, 123
  pheromone glands 122, 123
  tail wrapping 123
Tamyt (cat) 44
Tanny (kitten) 15–16
taste 85, 95–7
taurine 193
teeth 25–6, 34, 197–8
  hissing and 108
  kittens' 58, 64
  pain 147
  prehistoric 32, 33, 34
  tooth resorption 26
television 77, 81, 82, 218–19
temperament 51, 150–1, 189
temperature: body 28, 29, 98
  body language and 109
temple cats 44–5
territories 39, 47
  scent marks 120
  scratching and 132
  spray marking 127–8
  unburied faeces 130
theory of mind 154, 166–7
thermoregulation 27, 98
thinking like a cat 153–69
Thorndike, Edward 155–6
ticks 3–4
Tinbergen, Nikolaas 141
toe beans 19
toes 15, 17, 19–20

tomb paintings 43
tomcats: caterwauls 107–8
   social maturity 65
   spray marking 126, 127
   un-neutered 63–4, 123, 146
tongues 27
   taste buds 95, 96–7
tool use 165–6
touch 85, 98–100, 158
   whiskers 99–100
touch domes 19
training 160–5
Trap, Neuter and Return programmes
      (TNR) 174–5, 177, 178
trilling 106
Turner, Dennis C 155

U
Uexküll, Jakob Johann von 2–4
ultrasonic sounds 219
umwelt 2–4, 11, 95, 100
urination 126
   litter trays 192–3
   spraying 64
   urgent urination 135–6, 139
   urine marks 124, 125–9,
      132, 198
US, animal welfare in 188–9

V
vaccinations 206
valerian 91
vellus hairs 29
vertebrae 22–3
vestibular apparatus 24, 57
vets 148, 191, 210
   fear-anxiety of 145
   name association 158, 159–60
   smellscape of 121–2
vibrissae 29, 99–100
Vindolanda 46
viruses 197
vision 67–77

colour 72–3
   flicker factor 76–7
   focus 80–1
   movement and hunting 70–2, 73,
      218–19
   night and twilight 74–6
   visual field 71–2
vitamins 193–4
vocalizations 103–8, 118, 157
vomeronasal organ 93–4, 95
votive offerings 44

W
walking 17–18
water 27, 195, 214–15
weaning 55–6, 58, 59
welfare 9, 188
   companionship and conflict 198–201
   diet 193–5
   normal feline behaviour 195–8
   security and predictability 190–3
   UK legal requirements 188, 190, 193
Wells, Lis 177
whiskers 29, 69, 72, 99–100
wild cats 35, 172, 200
   African wildcats 35, 38, 39–40, 46, 47
   coat colour 37–8
   European wildcat 35
   food preferences 53, 58
   sociability 199
   Scottish wildcat 38
   vs. domestic cats 38
wildlife, free-roaming cats and 197, 217
worms 197
worship, cat 43–5
wriggles 21–2
Wynne, Clive 168–9

Y
yowling 108, 199

Z
zoomies 217–18

ACKNOWLEDGEMENTS

The authors would like to thank Professor Ron Ofri, Professor Matthias Laska, Professor Klaus Scherer, Dr Lauren Finka, Dr John Bradshaw, Dr Sarah Ellis, Trudi Atkinson, Vicky Halls, and all those whose help has enhanced this book, and who have contributed to furthering the knowledge and welfare of domestic cats.

PICTURE CREDITS